SAUNTERING

To Jerilyn,
From my heart
to yours —

Tom O-T
9/29/13

Also by Tom Owen-Towle:

Generation to Generation
Staying Together
New Men, Deeper Hungers
Spiritual Fitness
Brother-Spirit
The Gospel of Universalism
Friendship Chronicles

Sauntering

A Soul-Journey in the Woods with Thoreau as my Guide

by

Tom Owen-Towle

Bald Eagle Mountain Press
San Diego, California

For information, write to:
    Bald Eagle Mountain Press
    9985 Huennekens Street, Suite B
    San Diego, CA 92121

FIRST EDITION
ISBN 0-9630636-2-6

Dedication

To Lane Devereux, my soul-sister who introduced me to Dorland and undergirded this project with her cheers and critique, but never got to become a Dorland dweller herself due to health infirmities, I dedicate this book with admiration and appreciation for her manifold gifts and sustaining friendship.

Foreword

Thoreau said he required "of all writers, first or last, a simple and sincere account of their own lives, and not merely what they have heard of other lives." Tom Owen-Towle has followed Thoreau's lead in this, as in other things, and has given us, in *Sauntering,* a simple and sincere (and wise and useful) account of a modern spiritual journey.

It is part of our unappeasable hunger and restlessness as Americans that we so easily turn to the East or the ancients for guidance. Owen-Towle knows better, as did Thoreau. He knows that we may seek the whole world over only to come suddenly upon what we sought right here at home. Owen-Towle knows, as Thoreau knew, what or rather who it is we are really hunting with such avidity. "A man receives," Thoreau wrote, "only what he is ready to receive, whether physically or intellectually or morally. . . . We hear and apprehend only what we already half know. . . . Every man thus *tracks himself* through life, in all his hearing and reading and observation and travelling. His observations make a chain. The phenomenon or fact that cannot in any wise be linked with the rest which he has observed, he does not observe."

Owen-Towle's journey takes place in California, not Concord. What Thoreau discovered in Concord and Owen-Towle in California is that it is our caring about a place that makes it sacred. In the same way that Thoreau encountered himself at Walden, Owen-

Towle finds himself at Dorland Mountain Arts Colony, at Ticanu Pond, in a cabin called "Orchard House." Thoreau is a particularly good master because he does not require disciples, let alone clones. And Owen-Towle, in his title, claims not too much, but too little. He has learned, partly perhaps from Thoreau, to go in search of himself, and he has found a way to record his encounter so that the reader will be warmed and encouraged by the result.

This is a book about finding, or perhaps re-finding oneself. It is about how, in the middle of a busy, admirable public life, to get back to essentials, to tolerate silence and solitude, to see who really is at home there inside the spectacularly busy person of the world so many of us have turned into. Of course, we are haunted by the possibility that, by midlife, there may be nobody there at all. Most of us have a hunch that we had better keep up the busyness and blaze of our outer lives, rip through the mail, plot our trips, extend our lists of engagements, edge our lawns, clean our drapes, and attend our many meetings, morning, noon, and night.

Tom Owen-Towle takes off from Thoreau as he takes off from his own full life, to see who it is that is really there in the dark, in the long hours of stillness, in the novel and threatening solitude of a mountain hideaway. His account will hearten any reader who doubts that a month is long enough for real spiritual renewal or who doubts that renewal is even possible in a modern life lived largely at freeway speed.

Finally, Owen-Towle comes to his own conclusions, shaped by his wide reading and his own life. One can tell from his prose that he has earned his insights and applied his reading. "Style," said Whitehead, "is the ultimate morality of mind." Towards the end of this book, Owen-Towle quotes a wonderful passage from Annie Dillard. "We are here to witness," she writes. "There is nothing else to do with those mute materials we do not need. . . . We do not use the songbirds, for instance. We do not eat many of them; we cannot befriend them; we cannot persuade them to eat more mosquitoes or plant fewer weed seeds. We can only witness them." Owen-Towle comments–and the clean, spare style is the measure of his mind–"I am finally getting it through this thick skin and stubborn soul of mine that the point of life is primarily to show up, take our seats, and pay attention. The fundamental religious act is astonishment."

Tom Owen-Towle has shown up, taken his place, paid attention, expressed astonishment. Now it is our turn to listen to him.

Robert D. Richardson, Jr., author
Henry Thoreau, A Life of the Mind

Contents

Cover Illustration
"Forest Shadows"
by Millard Sheets, 1970

Chapter Illustrations
by Tony Sheets

Introduction

I went to the woods because I wished to live deliberately,
to front only the essential facts of life, and see if I could not
learn what it had to teach, and not, when I came to die,
discover that I had not lived.

Thoreau

In 1845, at the age of 28, Henry David Thoreau went to the
woods at Walden Pond, just two miles outside his home in Concord, Massachusetts, "to front only the essential facts of life." In
the final decade of the 20th century, at the age of 48, I left my
metropolitan haven to face certain fundamentals of my existence:
stillness, silence, darkness, nature, gods, demons, and angels.

I chose a mountainous area because I trusted wilderness would
drive me to depths unfrequented in the bustle of normal city life.
The woods could *educate*–literally "draw forth"–my soul in ways
consequential for the second half of my life. I would enjoy, as
Thoreau depicted in his Walden retreat, "my own sun and moon

and stars, and a little world all to myself."

With a month of sabbatical to spend, I might have been tempted to study in an academic setting at the feet of illustrious theologians and poets. Fortunately, I knew better. What I needed, at this point in my mid-life quest, was not more formal education, however stimulating, but a radical change of pace and scenery, far from seductive centers of ambition, where I could take spiritual stock, emptying myself of professional pressures and social obligations. I required sacred space and unscheduled time to search my soul, behold nature, and invite the transcendent — pursuits sorely neglected in my all-too-hectic existence as a parish minister.

I recalled reading a magazine article about the Dorland Mountain Arts Colony, a wilderness habitat in the Temecula Valley, an hour or so northeast of our San Diego home. Dorland provides a pristine, untrammeled Southern California refuge situated on the western boundary of the Palomar mountain range, bountiful with local wildlife, and punctuated by winding trails through chaparral and tree-dotted canyons. It is a working retreat for musicians, artists, and writers.

Ellen and Robert Dorland homesteaded these rustic 300 acres in the 1930s, and later donated the land to the Nature Conservancy (a private conservation group) with the stipulation that a renewal center for creative people be developed and sustained. So it has been since 1974.

Dorland furnishes six residents with private, Spartan-like cottages, but its main gift is uninterrupted time to deepen the spirit while enhancing one's craft. Nestled in the woods, without electricity and other amenities of urban life, Dorland would prove ideal for sauntering—burrowing inwardly into soul and gazing outwardly amidst nature.

Having applied for temporary residency, I was accepted for the month of February and I seized the opportunity.

My journey to Dorland furnished fascinating comparisons and contrasts with Thoreau's trek to Walden. His mid-19th-century pilgrimage, which has transformed millions of renowned and ordinary lives ever since, also influenced my modest sabbatical. Thoreau, while not my guru, remains one of my pivotal spiritual guides.

Thoreau retired for two years, two months, and two days into the Walden Pond surroundings. I lived near Ticanu (Indian for "water of everlasting youth") Pond for one month.

Thoreau was a New Englander, and I a Californian—my children being fourth-generation natives. We performed our respective soul-work on opposite coasts.

Thoreau built his own ten-foot-square cabin; I rented a larger cottage for $5 per day.

He and I both departed to the woods to write, but Thoreau logged ample time working the land, while I spent the bulk of my days and nights tilling fallow, inner terrain.

Thoreau regularly entertained friends, like Ralph Waldo Emerson, and crammed as many as 25 to 30 people inside his cabin at any given time. Much to my delight, we were disallowed visitors from the "outside world," and our sole communication with fellow Dorlandians was a communal message board. Most days I greeted only animals.

One of Thoreau's biographers notes, " . . . he would find no love that pure in human society, so he turned to nature." Thoreau preferred to "fall in love with the moon and the night, and find . . . love requited." On the contrary, I am more at home among people than animals or plants. Although I grow increasingly introspective with the years, I hardly resemble a recluse.

Neither Walden nor Dorland are menacing wilderness areas to be braved by rugged pioneers. Neither of us was Daniel Boone. Our journeys were symbolic adventures more than sustained ways of life. Thoreau called Walden an "experiment" and his visits with nature and soul "excursions"–apt descriptions for my trek as well. Richard Schneider in his volume *Henry David Thoreau* confirms this perspective:

> Thoreau is far enough from Concord to view it with some objectivity but is still involved in it enough not to abandon all subjective attachment to it. He is in the woods but not in the wilderness. His beanfield, we learn later, is a "half-civilized" field.

At Dorland I remained an urbanite enjoying a rustic change of pace. My soulful sabbath traversed, Buddha-like, the middle path between ascetic deprivation and self-indulgence—"half-civilized," as Thoreau observed.

Although we both took to the woods to regain spiritual equilibrium, Thoreau and I were hardly idle or passive. What with considerable walking and faithful writing, neither of us would qualify as a wastrel. In fact, it was a constant struggle to keep my legs and mind from too much activity. I tried, in my sojourn in the woods, to be disciplined, "to live deliberately" as Thoreau would say, without being driven. I wanted to entertain the serendipitous stream of this wondrous yet foreign realm.

Just as Thoreau sprinkled his immense literary legacy with occasional poems, so I have scattered haiku throughout this book. Haiku, of relatively recent Japanese origin (1899) and frequently used in Zen Buddhism, is an unrhymed verse form with three lines, composed usually of five, seven, and five syllables, respectively.

Haiku, clothed in plain raiment, accents the simple and commonplace. Nothing is too trifling to be its subject. I have grown fond of these terse, pliant, evocative morsels of poetic expression. Haiku has furnished an especially fitting and occasionally sublime medium to galvanize flashing, kaleidoscopic images from my excursions into nature and soul.

When Emerson remarked on the need for great poets, Thoreau said he had found one in the woods, but it had feathers on its body and had not yet matriculated to Harvard. "Let us cage it," said Emerson. "That is just the way the world always spoils its poets," responded Thoreau. And one might add, that is precisely how the world ruins its wilderness. In any case, haiku are not refined, caged pieces, but most convincing when wild and expansive.

Finally, Thoreau penned: "My purpose in going to Walden Pond was not to live cheaply nor to live dearly there, but to transact some private business with the fewest obstacles." My Dorland hermitage was likewise spent in transacting my own private business, that is, paying homage to the commodious cavities of my soul. I ponder an old Quaker greeting, "How is it with thy spirit?" The truth is that we hard-driving types don't slow down enough to answer that question.

The mature, abundant existence is marked by the capacity to probe directly both the far-flung cosmos and one's spacious inner universe. This is what Thoreau meant in his summons for humanity to "explore thyself." *Explore* is the correct term for soul-work, since it denotes a vigorous and thorough, yet open-ended search. Thoreau beckoned us to *explore*—not merely *know* or *trust*—thyself. The difference is striking. Explorers keep traveling beyond acquired wisdom and self-confidence. Equally at home amid discoveries and mysteries, true pilgrims journey ever onward, their quest unfinished even at death. Note the two faces of *thyself*: we are exhorted to explore the natural realm firsthand and to farm our own souls as well.

Sometimes these twin explorations—looking around and looking within—are overlapping pursuits. Naturalist John Muir confirmed this in his musing: "I only went out for a walk, and finally concluded to stay out till sundown for going *out*, I found, was really going *in*." Our soul may awaken precisely while we are tracking the woods, and interior investigation may thicken our ties with animals and trees, firmament and turf. In any case, both explorations are toilsome, sometimes unseasonably harsh. Bristling with thorns, beauty is strenuously achieved while exploring thyself. Both quests are inexhaustible as well, since more soul and nature always remain to be fathomed.

So I left for the Dorland Mountain Arts Colony with eagerness and trepidation. My wife Carolyn drove with me to the colony refuge, toured the premises awhile, then returned to San Diego. I felt deposited like a fledgling Boy Scout at base camp.

But I came prepared. I was equipped with thermal underwear (even Southern California's Februaries are chilly), alarm clock (although I ended up paying scant heed to either clock or watch), two flashlights, calamine lotion, binoculars, gloves with open fingers so I could write while shivering, and tweezers for splinter or tick removal.

I also brought along my Native American talking stick and Tibetan singing bowl as meditative catalysts. I left my guitar, radio, and typewriter at home, trusting the mellifluous sounds of nature to be sufficient provision.

I wasn't without niggling anxieties. I was worried about prowling animals, keeping warm, and the failure of any and all kerosene-operated pieces of equipment in my cottage. Thankfully, Dorland supplied a site manager to rescue mechanical dumbbells like me.

I had another fear. I had to guard against sabotaging my appointments with nature and soul by curling up with books next to a blazing fire. So I brought little to read and, armed with firm resolve, I avoided intellectual enticements until darkness prevailed. The bulk of my waking hours were spent honoring Thoreau's wilderness imperative: "Read not the *Times*. Read the Eternities."

But my most absorbing consternation had to do with what I

would find—or worse yet *not* find—during this earnest exploration inside my being. Perhaps I would become utterly bored, or discover my interior castle barren; worse yet, it might be filled to the brim with unpleasant beasties. I was about to find out.

It has proven comforting to know that countless pilgrims throughout human history made similar treks into the woods—soul-journeys, if you will. Jesus launched his ministry, at the age of thirty, by entering the wilderness to encounter existential temptations. The third stage of the Hindu's life is the invitation to be a "forest-dweller."

Even in Thoreau's own time there were excursions not unlike his own. In *Henry Thoreau: A Life of the Mind*, Robert D. Richardson, Jr. documents them as follows:

> Thoreau's was not a very adventurous move, certainly not when compared to other contemporary ventures, to Ellery Channing's sojourn on the Illinois prairie, to Melville's four years of seafaring, to Sir John Franklin's doomed efforts this same summer to sail from Greenland to the Pacific via the subarctic waters of Baffin Bay, or to the westward moving Mormons who left Nauvoo, Illinois, for Utah in 1846, or to John Charles Fremont, or to innumerable small groups such as the Donner party, which left Fort Bridger on the last day of July 1846, bound over the mountains to California. Thoreau was well aware that what he was doing was not braving wilderness, but simulating its conditions in a sort of symbolic or laboratory experiment.

Nonetheless, all soul-journeys ventured by us earthlings—whether short or long (the Japanese sage Kamo-No Chomei spent 30 years in his hut), whether relatively dangerous or safe—are admirable. Such pilgrimages are both emblematic and real. Humans make these journeys because we must; our souls wither without them. They expand our horizons and often transmute the very course of our tomorrows.

Thoreau at 28 and I at 48 made our respective trips at crossroads in our evolution. When you consider that at the turn of the 20th century, life-expectancy was 47 (in fact, Thoreau died at 44) and today it is 77, Thoreau and I both were navigating mid-life quests. There comes a critical juncture in our lives when we know indubitably that we have crossed over from the morning to the afternoon, to use Carl Jung's apt metaphor. He described this transition as follows:

> The afternoon of human life must also have a significance of its own and cannot be merely a pitiful appendage to life's morning. . . . We cannot live in the afternoon of life according to the program of life's morning—for what was great in the morning will be little in the evening, and what in the morning was true will at evening become a lie.

In the morning of life we conventionally develop outreach skills, we go forth to make good in the world, get educated, partnered, rear children, and care for older family members. But, as Jung relates, "whoever carries over into the afternoon the aims of the morning must pay for it with damage to the soul."

In the second half of life, or the afternoon, we hanker to search within, to know life more deeply, to inquire rather than acquire, to summarize our singular destinies, to locate sacred spaces for solitude and serenity, to enter the woods, figuratively or literally. This is what Jung unabashedly called "the religious outlook." All patients whom he saw in the second half of their lives were suffering from what he considered malaises of the soul.

In the afternoon of our human journeys, we cease looking for outside mentors, and realize that we, ourselves, are such. We slow down, take stock, behold trees and stars, make peace with our souls, and pare our life down to essentials. To use Thoreau's suggestive word for walking, we *saunter.* At Dorland my existence was spare, revolving around these constants: Owen-Towle, Thoreau, and Ticanu Pond.

In this book, I recall portions of Thoreau's sojourn at Walden Pond as well as my own stay at Dorland, but I mainly intend to inspire readers to plot their own quests. Whether venturing a few miles outside the village, meandering across the globe, or simply sitting in a quiet corner in the attic, our adventures must be custom made. Thoreau puts it pointedly:

> I would not have any one adopt *my* mode of living on any account; for, beside that before they have fairly learned it I may have found out another for myself, I desire that there may be as many different persons in the world as possible; but I would have all be very careful to find out and pursue *their own* way, and not their father's or mother's or neighbor's instead.

Our afternoon excursions will turn out to be as varied as we are. For example, Bert sequestered himself at the beach in his camper for two months. Helene attended a life-altering silent retreat at a Catholic monastery. Alex takes periodic hikes in the desert to restore his soul. Sally and her partner traveled across the country in their motorhome à la John Steinbeck in *Travels with Charley*. Catherine builds mini-sabbaticals into her year's work calendar.

But two elements are universally necessary: the willingness to gaze deep, deep within, and the openness to behold the boundless numinosity of the universe with keen eyes.

Chapter I

Solitude

"I thrive best on solitude"

After our late afternoon arrival, Dorland's coordinating fellow, Jane Culp, a visual artist, spends the better part of an hour stating the rules and teaching me how to keep my electricity-free cabin reasonably warm and adequately aglow with woodstove and lanterns. She gives Carolyn and me a tour of the refuge, pointing out the hiking trails, the spring-fed Ticanu Pond, the message center, the communal garden, and the Dorland library, and then wishes me blessed solitude.

Carolyn, sensitive to my mounting anxiety and the impending dark, embraces me lovingly, steers me back into my dank headquarters, and drives home. Thoreau may have thrived on solitude; at this point, I would settle for survival.

When the darkness slowly fills the valley, I turn on all available lanterns, cozy up next to the fire and dive into Annie Dillard's *The Writing Life;* I thirst for the kind of inspiration she has delivered during the past two decades. I don't progress beyond this melancholy passage: "When I came home in the middle of the night I was tired; I longed for a tolerant giant, a person as big as a house, to hold me and rock me."

Annie's plight is similar to mine; only the locales differed. She is retreating in Cape Cod; I, on the opposite shore, in the Southern California mountains. Our yearnings, however, are identical. It is no later than 7:00 p.m., yet I hanker for soothing comfort in the worst way, in the shape of a person, smaller than myself, "to hold me and rock me." Carolyn is her name. By 8:00 p.m. or so, it hits me that conjugal visits will clearly be off limits at Dorland during the month of February.

I read a bit longer, down some orange slice candies (a love gift Carolyn secretly nestled in my pack), put on warm socks, don my thermal underwear and nightshirt, and then, after turning out the lanterns and testing my penlight, I climb deep down under a mound of covers, and sleep fitfully for ten hours.

At 6:30 a.m., the darkness has lifted. Five semi-wild cats are making a ruckus outside my cabin, Orchard House. I am unable to hide out any longer. Clambering in slow motion, I join the noisy throng, and the six of us head out together on the trail to Far Spring.

"Explore the private sea"

It is easier to sail many thousands of miles through cold and storm and cannibals, in a government ship, with five hundred persons to assist one, than it is to explore the private sea, the Atlantic and Pacific Ocean of one's being alone.

Thoreau

Dorland is rustic acreage basically uncorrupted by civilization. It furnishes a perfect setting for "exploring the private sea" of my soul.

Privacy is a rare treasure indeed, and once we modern folks possess some, we tend to ignore it, squander it, or race to fill it up. Being apart from observation or company, secluded, free from unauthorized intrusions is a far cry from life today. We seldom stop talking and producing long enough to find out what we truly believe and cherish. As Dag Hammarskjöld lamented: "Too tired for company, we seek a solitude we are too tired to fill."

Being *private* is a state distinct from being *personal.* Americans are trained to be cordial and gregarious. We grow close to others, often with ease and alacrity. We are personal, yet few of us have a working acquaintanceship with our solitariness. My hunch is we are scared of what we might uncover. So we are safely "personal" with others to avoid being intimately "private" with ourselves. Again, Thoreau cuts to the quick of our 20th-century mentality when he contends:

> In proportion as our inward life fails, we go more con-
> stantly and desperately to the post-office. You may depend
> on it, that poor fellow who walks away with the greatest
> number of letters, proud of his extensive correspondence,
> has not heard from himself this long while.

The truth remains: unless we begin to cultivate our private sides, our personalities shrivel from malnutrition. We must learn to pay serious, ongoing attention to our privacy without becoming isolates, navigating an ennobling sea in quest of spiritual fulfillment.

Alone does not mean lonely

If you ask yourself when was the last time you were totally alone, solitary as a jaybird perched in an empty tree, you would probably be hard pressed to say.

Even if you live alone, you are visited continually by phone calls, TV personalities, neighbors, colleagues, mail carriers, salespeople, and more. Take a head count of all the human contacts you've made—wanted or unwanted—during the past 24 hours, and you will be startled.

Dorland is the first chosen, extended block of time during my adulthood where I alone am privileged to shape the substance and order of my agenda. The Colony permits no outside intrusions, pressures, dictates, collaboration. I am essentially living unhampered and unaided by the customary accoutrements of civilization.

As short as one month is (and February *is* the shortest), it could seem an eternity to one as uninitiated as I in the mysteries of solitude. Oscar Wilde, the Irish writer, confessed he could never become a Socialist because he liked to keep his evenings free.

Most of us in the "helping" professions are people addicts. We clergy are notorious offenders, working into the wee hours of most nights, unscrambling problems of the universe or people. We cringe at being left alone, untouched, underappreciated, unproductive; so we, unlike Wilde, book our evenings solid in order to avoid hours of lonesomeness.

I acquired this malady early on in my profession. After all, as Dorothy Parker used to jest, "People are more fun than anybody." So they are, more fun and far needier. Being somewhat suspicious, even fearful, of my own solitude, I envisioned my mission in ministry was essentially to protect others from their aloneness.

When there are worthwhile things to accomplish in the vineyards of the Lord, and human beings to serve or save, solitude can seem an unnecessary luxury, perhaps a waste of time. Nevertheless, a spiritual pilgrim as astute as Blaise Pascal chides us in *Pensées* that "All of our misfortunes spring from the single cause that we are unable to stay quietly in one room."

Needless to say, Dorland is doing its damnedest to turn me "outside in." Inexorably, I am acclimating to my aloneness, becoming more at home in my inner residence, finding moments of solitude gradually less terrifying. I am recognizing that being *alone* is not equatable with being *lonely* and that, on the contrary, the former abets my every effort to diminish the latter.

The truth is that human creatures are restless when racing compulsively from pillar to post; only when we drink leisurely from the wellsprings of solitude do we bring impressive, durable resources to either our vocations or companions.

Tempted to cheat

In Woody Allen's movie "Annie Hall," the protagonist says: "I was thrown out of New York University for cheating on a metaphysics exam. The professor caught me looking deeply into the soul of the student seated next to me."

At Dorland, even in my braver moments, I am sorely tempted to stare into everyone else's soul but my own: Annie Dillard's, Loren Eiseley's, Alice Walker's, Wendell Berry's or Denise Levertov's; any one of the other Dorland artists ensconced in their own private business; even the rowdy cats meowing on my roof.

If I were desperate enough, I could bury myself in my car, turn the radio on, and bask in the decibels of American civilization. But Dorland is a driving taskmaster, and so is Thoreau's relentless admonition to "explore thyself," to "explore the private." Nonetheless, I cheat a little, because I plaster the walls and floors of my cabin with written imperatives from other solitary questors, all promoting the interior hunt. Their wisdom emboldens this reluctant adventurer.

Without great solitude, no serious work is possible.

Pablo Picasso

Only when one is connected to one's own core is one connected to others . . . and, for me, the core, the inner spring, can best be refound through solitude.

Anne Morrow Lindbergh

By all means use sometimes to be alone. Salute thyself: see what thy soul doth wear. Dare to look in thy chest; for 'tis thine own. And tumble up and down what thou find'st there.

George Herbert

Solitude is employing the richness of self. Loneliness is facing the poverty of self.

May Sarton

Nobody can counsel and help you, nobody. There is only one single way. Go into yourself.

Rainer Maria Rilke

Never am I less alone than when I am by myself; never am I more active than when I am doing nothing.

Cato

Being solitary is being alone well. Being alone luxuriously immersed in doings of your own choice, aware of the fullness of your own presence rather than of the absence of others. Because solitude is an achievement.

Alice Koller

And now, the best of all, is to be alone, to possess one's soul in silence.

D. H. Lawrence

Thus saith the Lord God, the Holy One of Israel: in returning and rest shall you be saved; in quietness and confidence shall be your strength.

Isaiah 30:15

Dorland, oh Dorland, keep insisting that I look long and lovingly into my chest, to see what my soul doth wear!

"A simple and sincere account"

I should not talk so much about myself if there were anybody else whom I knew as well. Unfortunately, I am confined on this theme by the narrowness of my experience. Moreover, I, on my side, require of all writers, first or last, a simple and sincere account of their own lives, and not merely what they have heard of other lives.

Thoreau

It has been a venerable male proclivity to write abstractly rather than confessionally. Theology is the most grievous culprit, being a discipline dominated, until recent times, by men who have flourished in pulpits six feet above contradiction, majoring in esoteric ruminations and lofty edicts.

Thoreau pulls us crashing back to earth, to "simple and sincere accounts" of what is happening in our very own lives. "Explore thyself," he exhorts, "explore thyself," then report your learnings.

The Sufi fable tells of a seeker after enlightenment who sets out on a pilgrimage to a distant destination. Not finding wisdom at the end of her journey, she disappointedly returns home, and, lo and behold, discovers that the treasure so ardently sought elsewhere lies within her own abode, more specifically, in her own soul.

Maybe that's why Thoreau seldom traveled far from home,

holding that truth dwelt wherever he did. "It is not worth the while to go round the world to count the cats in Zanzibar," he announced, being disenthralled with straying from either Concord or his soul.

Thoreau proposed that, once life's dust settles, the only odyssey worth relating is our own. Our human mission is no more complicated than transmitting our stories in simple and sincere fashion. If we were all brave enough to do that, humanity would be the beneficiary of a splendid treasure trove. As Lao Tse noted: "Understanding others is wisdom; understanding yourself is enlightenment."

Consequently, the core of my Dorland experience consists in reading nature and my soul rather than devouring outsiders, however tantalizing and delectable. "Explore thyself" and uncover wellsprings of illimitable refreshment.

Different countries

There are the lover and the beloved, but these two come from different countries.

Carson McCullers

Despite periodic professional junkets, Carolyn and I have always lain in one another's arms on February 14th, in the nearly two decades of our loving partnership. Not so, this Valentine's Day.

But a mere 75 miles apart, we reside in different countries—Dorland and San Diego, the woods and the metropolis, spiritually foreign lands to each other. In her country, Carolyn is avalanched daily with urgent tasks and important people. In my territory, I am deluged with 24 hours of serenity.

Even our Valentine's cards, oozing with the kind of erotic sentiment lavished from afar, misfire this year. Mine arrives late, and Carolyn's is returned: "Not deliverable at this address." Anything that insinuates its way into Dorland's "working retreat for creative people" is apparently self-generated and hand-carried.

Thus, my sauntering in solitude provides not only a challenge for the soul, but also a test for the suppleness of our marriage.

Being alone in the woods preoccupies my mind with perturbing questions: How long can I comfortably live apart from my mate? Does absence strengthen or diminish our bond? What if either of us experiences greater fulfillment dwelling by ourselves? Sensitive, imaginative thinkers throughout history have grappled mightily with the elusive interplay between aloneness and intimacy. Their unanimous verdict: we require both in overlapping tension.

Trapped in one of life's existential ruts, some of us idealize solitude, while others romanticize love. Foolishly, we exalt one value to the exclusion of the other. Yet both apartness and eros are holy forces, agonizingly intertwined in robust human lives.

Any love-bond seeks its singular, suitable rhythm in the dance of intimacy and independence. What complicates matters is the presence of two utterly distinct and valued partners bringing their diverse training, anxieties, steps, and yearnings to the floor.

Sometimes the choreography grows even more intricate. We dancers are surrounded by a host of bystanders, usually well-meaning, gawking, evaluating our every movement, and therewith rating our love. When the scorecards are raised, it is difficult for us, dancers on stage, to disregard the numbers, and trust that only insiders truly appreciate the soundness and flaws of our particular swirl around life's ballroom.

Nonetheless, lovers never cease the dance, believing that if we hold one another too tightly, the juices might drain away—yet, if we gambol too loosely, either of us might wheel out of our beloved's reach. What constitutes, then, the right style, mood, tempo, and proximity to make our personalized movements a dance, not merely bodies milling or smothering? All Carolyn and I know is that our love is heartiest and healthiest when we keep such imponderables alive.

By now, our mutual, enduring affection has been established. Our emotional fracases with one another are also a part of our personal history. Our persistent vow—to stay together for better, for worse—is renewed daily. Yet, our marital adventure never gets any easier. Intractable, stubborn challenges keep coming and going and arriving again.

We still valiantly attempt to discern how our separate beings, our two realities might move alongside one another joyfully, with walls down, amid full-force equality and ample dialogue, while simultaneously respecting our necessary boundaries and peculiar habits.

Like all lovers, we dwell in adjacent yet different countries.

"A few moments"

It is a great relief when for a few moments in the day we can retire to our chamber and be completely true to ourselves. It leavens the rest of our hours.

Thoreau

The butterfly counts not months but moments, and has time enough.

Rabindranath Tagore

We can rationalize our way into avoidance of solitude, claiming that if we are unable to retreat for a year, a month, or even a weekend, we might as well spurn the practice altogether. But the length of our forays into aloneness is not at stake; seizing "a few moments" alone, daily, can keep our souls sufficiently awake and fit.

Great interest surrounded the start of Jesus' ministry—40 days in the wilderness—and its close—a lonely vigil in the garden—but we forget that the Nazarene prophet took mini-sabbaths all along the way. The New Testament recounts Jesus withdrawing from life's tumult on a regular basis: "And when he had sent the multitude away, Jesus went up into a mountain apart to pray; and when the evening was come, he was there alone" (Matthew 14:23).

Solitude is not so much a cup to replenish as a stream to experience. Solitude is a state that may be visited whether we are energetic or bushed, ready to give birth or prepared to enter one's final night.

But four rules obtain: one, since we are always too busy, we must pluck opportunities to be alone; two, there is seldom the wrong time to explore solitude; three, we need "to lean into solitude" (Denise Levertov's image) rather than skirt lazily on its edge; and four, a few moments is enough to refresh our souls.

"Three chairs"

> I had three chairs in my house; one for solitude, two for friendship, three for society.
>
> Thoreau

The three chairs in Thoreau's tiny cabin were frequently occupied. He had plenty of visitors, to be sure, yet he would carefully protect his independence even amid the throng, heeding the spiritual counsel of his closest friend, and customary Walden visitor, Ralph Waldo Emerson:

> It is easy in the world to live after the world's opinion; it is easy in solitude to live after our own, but the great person is one who in the midst of the crowd keeps with perfect sweetness the independence of solitude.

Maintaining his equilibrium was a constant concern for Thoreau: "I have had 25 or 30 souls, with their bodies, at once under my roof, and yet we often parted without being aware that we had come very near to one another."

Intimacy, Thoreau contended, was not directly correlated with proximity. Human beings could be physically juxtaposed (or jammed together in the case of the 30 bodies in his modest cabin) without being emotionally close and vice versa. To further complicate matters, being *by* myself doesn't mean I will be *with* myself. We creatures are exasperatingly ingenious at creating ways to escape our deeper selves.

My trip to Dorland was an excursion to be not merely alone, but meaningfully alone, to stay in intimate alignment with myself without drifting off into my "monkey mind" (the picturesque Zen Buddhist phrase for mental clutter), hiding from the illuminations and blemishes of my soul.

Despite frequent visitors and periodic trips home for his mother's home-cooking, Thoreau was a loner. He could honestly report: "I never found the companion that was so companionable as solitude." He was never as comfortable with society—its dictates and resources—as he was with nature or his own company. Emerson accurately conferred on his associate "the bachelor of thought and nature." Bachelor in both senses of the term: diploma recipient and unmarried man.

My quandary differs from Thoreau's. Feeling more at home in society, I have less need for visitors during my retreat than he did. At Ticanu Pond I entertain nobody. I shun people. When one of the cats recently scooted into my cabin, I chased it out. Only the rats race around in Orchard House, day and night, and that's because I can't get rid of them.

I retreated to Dorland for one overarching reason: to befriend my solitariness, so that when I leave the woods I might relish holier moments apart and alone. An ironic bonus follows. Being secluded for a month from social tumult and fury, brings me closer not only to myself but to others as well, in a healthy, less symbiotic way. My controlling instincts are fading, a sense of perspective is gained, the well of affection for those nearest and dearest to me is refilled.

So, at Orchard House, I occupy my three chairs differently than Thoreau did. One is for meditation, sitting still. Two is for writing. Three is for night reading. It remains absolutely critical, at this delicate juncture in my spiritual blossoming, that "my soul hath elbow room" (William Shakespeare) and that I be "the Soul that has a Guest" (Emily Dickinson).

I share a soulful of company in this small cottage. My chairs are amply filled by me, myself, and I.

"Employment enough"

> I want to go soon and live away by the pond, where I shall hear only the wind whispering among the reeds. It will be success if I shall have left myself behind. But my friends ask what I will do when I get there. Will it not be employment enough to watch the progress of the seasons?
>
> Thoreau

To leave my pressured, driven self behind in uptown San Diego, if accomplished, would make my entire sojourn in the woods valuable. This is my elemental Dorlandian goal: to shed my burdened being and don a lighter one.

Some of my friends, not the least of whom is my own self, are fidgety about how I might pass the long, cool, dark February days in a cabin void of electricity and entertainment. To be sure, there are times when I want to slam shut the cabin door and bolt for home, but pluck and promises stay me on course. There are days during this Dorlandian experiment when my soul can't even work up a sweat. My mouth tastes as arid as weeds in the Temeculan meadows. My soul's thirst goes unwatered. Yet I keep sauntering amid solitude; I weather the spells of dryness.

The motif of "employment" recurs in Thoreau's writings, because he was consistently reprimanded by friends and foes alike for appearing lazy and indolent, unwilling to shoulder his fair share in the marketplace. However, his objective was never to earn a livelihood but to shape a life—"to affect the quality of the day, this is the highest of arts." Henry David Thoreau was interested not in cash but meaning, and who could fault him for fashioning a mission to fit the size of his spirit, then persevering to fulfill it?

Even when Thoreau left Walden he maintained a self-styled pace. He was satisfied to work 6 weeks per year for money and explore life the other 46 weeks: sauntering, "watching the progress of the seasons," and producing 3 million words of some of the finest prose and poetry in American literature. He was hardly loafing.

Thoreau humorously mused that the Bible had matters backwards and recommended this formula instead: work one day and rest the other six. "Rest" allowed him to busy himself with what he did best. He pointedly declared:

> If I should sell both my forenoons and afternoons to society, as most appear to do, I am sure that for me there would be nothing left worth living for. I trust that I shall never thus sell my birthright for a mess of pottage.

Well, he kept his pledge. He never sold his birthright once in 44 years. Rather he made daily expeditions into nature and worked his soul full-time.

Sounds like "employment enough."

"Fitted for a higher society"

You think that I am impoverishing myself, by withdrawing
from people, but in my solitude I have woven for myself a
silken web or chrysalis, and nymph-like, shall ere long burst
a more perfect creature, fitted for a higher society.

Thoreau

When I leave my Dorland sanctuary and return to the rigors
of valley existence, my fervent prayer is that the inner solitude I
attain in the woods will be re-created during my work day, in the
corners of my home, on the road, while at play—wherever I live,
move, and have my being.

May my spiritual repose be a moveable feast.

The purpose of retreating is to cultivate the soul, then return
renewed, "fitted for a higher society," prepared to participate
afresh in the creation of a lovelier, loftier commonweal.

Solitary pieces

Blessed solitude
Voice crying in wilderness:
"Start saving yourself!"

Different drummers
Life is drawn, written, scored here
Soul's naked bounty

Open-air confession
Unburdening to nature
Wind draws wounds away

Dry pen, mind sputters
Subterranean doubts gnaw
Mountains dance alone

Talking to myself
No mental aberration
Indispensable

When humans depart
Conversations do not cease
Deep-down voices take charge

I came with thin soul
Thickened on dark mysteries
And empty stretches

Too long, too short—both
My Dorlandian sojourn
Hard to leave or stay

Chapter II

Silence

Silence alone is worthy to be heard. Silence is of a various depth and fertility, like soil.

Thoreau

"A broad margin"

I love a broad margin to my life.

Thoreau

Once the Japanese emperor Hirohito was driven to a meeting hall for a scheduled appointment. When he arrived, no one was there. The Emperor strolled into the middle of the grand hall, stood silently for several moments, then bowed to the empty space.

He smiled, then told his assistants, "We must arrange more appointments like this. I haven't enjoyed myself so much for a long time."

Hirohito personifies the Asian fondness for quiet inactivity.

Each day, at Dorland, I am granted a shapeless ball of clay to mold. The next 24 hours are entirely mine. No one will visit or call me. No one will make demands upon my time, talent, or energy. I am immersed in silence. My soul and body, mind and heart are my only mates. Never has the margin of my adult life been so broad.

I bow to the cosmos and its abundance of teeming wildlife. I bow to my timid yet valorous soul. I bow to the Creator who birthed earth's extravagance into being. I bow, trembling, in gratitude.

Pondering

But Mary treasured up all these things and pondered over them.

"Who is the you or self who entered life in the first place?" The question was posed by African-American theologian Thandeka, whose name, meaning "gift of God," was bestowed by Bishop Desmond Tutu. The occasion was the "World-Centered Self" conference sponsored by the Beyond Racism Task Force at our church. Thandeka was pushing us to recall the spiritual being who, at our origin, was essentially innocent and unformed. Her conviction is that women and men do not catapult full-blown into existence as fearful or judgmental creatures.

Thandeka also invited us to revisit our earliest memories, and then, if possible, go back even further than that. She asked us to remember our first photographs—"stills" that caught our primal essence. Then we exchanged notes with one another in small groups.

My photograph was of a serene, pensive little guy, with golden-brown curls, nestled in a red wagon. I say serene because I appeared quite centered and secure; pensive because there seemed to be a lot weighing on my heart. "Future monk" was written all over my countenance.

I played back this memory to my mother, and she verified

the portrait: "Yes, Tom, you were unusually reserved as a baby, even as a youngster. You were shy and slower than most boys your age. Why, you didn't walk until you were 16 months old, and you hardly spoke until 4 or 5 years of age. Your father and I were concerned but hopeful that you were brooding over important things, biding your time."

Four decades later I view my childhood reticence with admiration. I mute the more loquacious self I have fervently cultivated since adolescence and reclaim vestiges of my original demeanor.

On my final laps around life's course, I hope to marry the contemplative and the productive, the forthright and the reticent areas of my being. To be a reflective activist is my destination.

I desire to be whole.

Entering the silence

Put your ear close down to your soul and listen hard.

Anne Sexton

My wife practices a long, family-honored tradition of "entering the silence." When Carolyn needs to be quiet and apart, like mother and grandmother before her, she warns all those nearby: "I love you, and I am entering the silence: a realm of sealed lips, closed eyes, and calm soul. In my own time, and not before, I will return to be with you."

Buddha entered the silence too. Huston Smith recounts Gautama's determined yet wrenching decision to leave behind the lure of the palace life and become a forest-dweller.

One night in his twenty-ninth year Buddha made the break, his Great Going Forth. Making his way in the post-midnight hours to where his wife and son were locked in sleep, he bade them both a silent goodbye, then ordered the gatekeeper to bridle his great white horse. The two mounted and rode off toward the forest. Reaching its edge by daybreak, Gautama changed clothes with the attendant who returned with the horse to break the news, while Gautama shaved his head and "clothed in ragged raiment" plunged into the forest in search of enlightenment. Six years followed during which his full energies were concentrated toward this end. "How hard to live the life of the lonely forest-dweller...to rejoice in solitude. Verily, the silent groves must bear heavy upon the monk who has not yet won to fixity of mind!" The words bear poignant witness that his search was not easy.

"Entering the silence" is a holy vow available to be taken by all God's creatures—women, men, and children. Animals and plants too. Some among us will make of our silence an honored profession; for most, it will consist of periodic respites or sojourns.

The Greek root *mys* in the words "mystery" and "mystic" means shutting the eyes, ears, or mouth because, in the presence of wondrous and awful things, we are driven to silence. The sacred enterprise summons us to be mute and dumb sometimes, to still our mouth, then our mind, finally our will—to shut up fully before we dare to open up freshly. It calls us to enter the silence, so the mystery within us might connect with the mystery beyond us.

"Precisely nothing"

Nature's silence is its one remark, and every flake of world is a chip off that old mute and immutable block. The Chinese say that we live in the world of ten thousand things. Each of the ten thousand things cries out to us precisely nothing.

Annie Dillard

I rise about 6:30 a.m. every morning at Dorland, put on my sweatsuit, woolen gloves, scarf and cap, and dawdle out into the bracing February chill. Shady, Dorland's camp dog, half-German Shepherd and half-wolf, ambles off with me on an hour-long winding junket through the low mountains of Southern California.

It is good to have a companion, especially a speechless one. I'm not interested in conversation; I haven't talked to people in days. Even Shady's sudden barks make disquieting noises and unnerve me. Grown accustomed to silence, my head turns with every bird chirp. I am beginning to appreciate "nature's silence . . . its one remark."

Upon return, I enter Orchard House, my citadel of silence, build a roaring fire, pull my chair and working paraphernalia up tight, and become small and subdued. This poses an unusual discipline for an industrious, modern male trained to loom large and full of utterance.

Before I set my mind into motion, I ring my Tibetan singing

bowl several times to center myself. To be fiercely attentive to the sounds of nature and soul is my occupation this month. Soul and nature, nature and soul in cadenced measure constitute my focus. And I meditate upon Thoreau's similar devotion:

> It is the marriage of the soul with Nature that makes the intellect fruitful, that gives birth to imagination.

"Silence is audible"

As the truest society approaches always nearer to solitude, so the most excellent speech finally falls into Silence. Silence is audible to all, at all times, and in all places.

Thoreau

In the mystical tradition, it is said: "Before the Word, there was silence." Before creation, before proclamation, and before chaos . . . there is silence.

We cannot hear humans talk, let alone "most excellent speech," unless there is silence. The more complete the silence, the more expressive the speech. Therefore, after any powerful outpouring of words, we welcome absolute quiet, rather than thunderous clapping—hardly our noblest human response to being stirred. There is no gratitude comparable to the gift of appreciative silence.

"Silence is audible . . . ." In the presence of exquisite art, the stillness of an unstirring forest, the quietude of the vast desert, the solemnity of the majestic mountains, the tranquility of gently falling snow, the ocean when waves are resting; in the face of unspeakable tragedy or the ineffable wonder of human love; in the presence of all these and much more, silence resounds. As the Psalmist declares: "There is no speech, nor are there words . . . yet their voice goes out" (Psalm 19:3).

I know why Thoreau capitalizes "Silence."

My hermitage

When your tongue is silent, you can rest in the silence of the forest. When your imagination is silent, the forest speaks to you, tells you of its unreality and of the Reality of God. But when your mind is silent, then the forest suddenly becomes magnificently real and blazes transparently with the Reality of God.

Thomas Merton

Orchard House has become my February hideaway. It even qualifies as a hermitage of sorts. However, it isn't hermetic, that is, sealed, airtight, or impervious to external influences. There are other fellows on the premises of Dorland and critters galore who stomp away on my roof like a thundering herd, especially during the nights. They are affectionately known around these parts as the "roof rhinos of Orchard House."

Dorland is about as close as I will ever come to the cloisters of monastic life. Governed most of my adult existence by the model of "knight," I have engaged in various enterprises, physical and spiritual alike, to display my prowess. Now, at mid-life, I choose to be something of a hermit, retiring from society, however briefly, for religious reasons. I am stalking my soul.

My mouth is tiny now, but my ears are big, just like the Buddha's. I have temporarily abandoned my cozy comforts—family, work, and society—for a novel, scarier set of companions: quiet, darkness, solitude, and nature. In these woods, one of my muddled, clumsier friendships—namely with God—is rigorously being revised. Sadly, my ministerial appointment book, back in the city, is usually too packed to make time, "quality" time as we clergy like to say, with Yahweh.

Yet in the forest, while I am alone and quiet, there is expectancy, for God moves nimbly in both worlds of community and nature. In surrendering to silence, we open ourselves to the holy. Black Elk has said that the true power of retreat is connection with silence, "for is not silence the very voice of the Great Spirit?"

But am I becoming a professional hermit? Not at all. My wife half-jokingly says that if I find myself favoring the life of a recluse, then I should just stay in the forest and not bother to come home. Actually, I am visiting the woods on a soul-journey, with no plans to take up permanent residence here. Once Thoreau, who spent 26 months at Walden Pond, came upon a man in the woods of Northern Maine, who had completely withdrawn from civilization. This professional hermit so flustered Thoreau, that Henry kept right on moving ahead.

Koviashuvik

> We liked everybody we met on the West Coast, even though
> we did not really meet anyone. We did not really meet
> anyone because everyone we met was coping. We could
> not talk with them the way we talk with people in the bush,
> which is what they call the wilderness where we live at
> Koviashuvik.
>
> Sam Wright

Koviashuvik is the Eskimo word meaning "time and place of joy in the present moment." It is the name Sam and Billie Wright bequeathed their wilderness home. This couple spent almost two decades above the arctic circle in the Brooks Range of Alaska, living in "the last major wilderness on the North American continent."

Sam tells me that it was so quiet sometimes at Koviashuvik that Billie could hear him returning to their 12-foot–square log cabin from nearly two miles away. Silence, embedded in their bones and souls, had become a veritable way of being.

On leave once, they were dining with friends in a small, quiet, off-the-beaten track restaurant in the Bay Area. The "deafening roar" of dishes and conversation catapulted Sam and Billie from their seats, and they scurried to vacate the diner.

Rick Bass, in his novelistic reflections upon a remote region of Montana, writes:

One old woman, whom everyone calls Grandma, has lived up here all her life. Eighty years in the Yaak. Think of all the things she has missed. But think of all the things she has seen that the rest of the world has missed. No one can get it all, no matter where they are.

Most Americans live amid tumultuous clamor and are hardly fazed. We have grown accustomed to a pathogenic noisiness that breeds agitation and aggression. Our culture, drenched in noise, deafens the mind to the inner voice, blunts our bedrock kinship with the subtle sounds of nature. We are so busy coping with bombast and hubbub that we fail to relish life's delicacies like silence—one of the magnificent legacies of Koviashuvik, Yaak, and my Dorland.

The Great Silence

As I leave the village, drawing nearer to the woods, I listen from time to time to hear the hounds of Silence baying the Moon—to know if they are on the track of any game. If there's no Diana in the night, what is it worth? I hark the goddess Diana. The silence rings; it is musical and thrills me. A night in which the silence was audible. I hear the unspeakable.

Thoreau

Over all the hilltops
Silence,
Among all the treetops
You feel hardly
A breath moving.
The birds fall silent in the woods.
Simply wait! Soon
You too will be silent.

Goethe

I'm a slow learner, but I finally acknowledge silence to be a substance not a vacuum. Silence is a reality; audible, as Thoreau reiterates. Silence exists. It is a presence rather than an absence, especially when nighttime arrives.

At approximately 5:00 p.m., it gets dark here in the Palomar mountains. My lanterns make a dent, but I feel roundly wrapped in darkness and its accompanying mysteries. At night, the silence seems denser, more palpable than during daylight. Without straining, I take in nonhuman sounds—eerie animal noises, crackling fire, wind-caused rattling—but mainly I listen intently to the silence. Its exceptional sounds remind me I am alone yet not completely alone.

In the monastic tradition, they call this time from dusk to dawn the "Great Silence." Between the last evening recreation and first morning meditation you are required to be quiet. I have gone on Catholic-guided retreats and know this practice firsthand.

Native American author Nancy Wood honors the "Great Silence" with this meditative blessing:

> It is our quiet time.
> We do not speak, because the voices
>   are within us.
> It is our quiet time.
> We do not walk, because the earth is all
>   within us.
> It is our quiet time.
> We do not dance, because the music
>   has lifted us
> to a place where the spirit is.
> It is our quiet time.
> We rest with all of nature. We wake
>   when the seven
> sisters wake.
> We greet them in the sky over the
>   opening of the kiva.

Great Silence: great with limitless meanings, great with sleep composed of respite and restlessness, and great with demons of the dark. Great also, because in our dreams the gods and goddesses are likely to visit us, knowing we are vulnerable, at home, unoccupied.

The Great Silence intimidates contemporary folks. It scares us, so we rush to fill this stretch of time with social busyness, bodies, drink, TV, and miscellaneous inanities instead of mustering courage to embrace the hushed void.

Befriending the Great Silence is one of my aspirations during life's "afternoon." I want to explore its consecrated, albeit terrifying, chambers, entertain its peculiar sounds without drowning them in human-made clatter. I also want to feel equally comfortable entering the Great Silence with or without loved ones by my side. Because, one day, when I cross over into my final silence—the ultimate darkness—I want to be spiritually seasoned.

Chapter III

Stillness

Let our souls catch up

What are you worth when motionless?

St. Exupéry

It's one thing to be alone, another to be quiet, yet a third to be *still*. Even as I write, I am moving; my right hand pushes a pencil on lined paper. I am sedentary but hardly static. My brain is eddying and so is my hand. My soul and body keep moving in the woods because I have trouble sitting still. My worth seems riveted on activity. Not surprisingly, I have succumbed to the prejudice that an energetic, bustling mind is the hallmark of a vital human being.

While I did select Dorland over an academic setting, I didn't choose inertia. I have entered the woods to muse, saunter, chant, meditate, and—yes, I confess—make notes on all that. To accomplish something. But changes are inexorably creaking in my soul. I am befriending stillness, fully aware that Thoreau could stand, unflappably still, for eight hours at a crack beside a pond, while admiring young frogs or observing duck eggs hatching.

Every day I climb to the summit of a nearby hill and sit overlooking the gorgeous canyons and valleys. I turn off my body and mind and just sit, motionless.

In the early evening I stare languorously at the flame of a candle, calm my galloping imagination, and go mindless. Whenever I squabble with stillness, which is my wont, I recollect with smiling heart the profundity of the following African tale.

A trader docked his ship in an African port and hired the natives to carry goods inland on their backs for bartering with other indigenous people for their produce. Day after day he got the people up early and walked them until late at night, always thinking of how much more profit he could make, if he could shorten the time that his boat stood empty in the harbor.

One morning he got up and found the transporters sitting quietly in a circle. The trader urged them to get up quickly and get started down the trail, but no one moved. After a long pause, the leader of the group announced, "We're going to sit still and wait until our souls catch up with our bodies!"

The story ends with the Africans still sitting still. As my life unfolds before me, I plan to grant my soul more time, as long as it takes, to catch up with my rambling body. Sitting still for stretches while at Dorland is a beginning.

"The grace of being still"

There are tidings from the Eternal Spirit who is not far away from any of us; tidings that will come and go unnoticed, unless we have won the grace of being still.

George Herbert Morrison

Teach us to care and not to care. Teach us to sit still.

T. S. Eliot

My soul-brother Michael has made for me a replica of the Native American "talking stick" from the natural elements of the San Diego area. Shaking the stick indicates a willingness to "speak one's truth." On one side of the rattle is an imaginative depiction of open, aspiring hands in yellow, black, white, and red—the colors of the four directions. On the other side are father-sky and mother-earth, intertwined in an explosive, healing dance.

I shake the stick whenever my confidence flags, to activate yet more wisdom born of tears, stillness, eros, anguish, and ecstasy. I shake it today and these unembellished truths tumble forth.

- Action is not the only anti-depressant. Being still and knowing I don't have to achieve in order to be accepted is sufficient medicine to chase despondency away.

- Could it be that my current case of "boredom" indicates I am resisting something important? Stay on target, push the block, keep boring . . .

- What's my rush? Whom am I racing? Walk, don't run. Be quiet, don't chatter. Stay alone, don't cling to people. Be still, don't flail.

- The octogenarian President of Mitsubishi Motors was asked about his company's future: "How long, Sir, are your long-range plans?" "Oh, about 250 years, he responded. "Then we'll go from there."

  Be still, and place things in perspective.

- Two complementary insights:

  "Be still and know that I am God." (Psalm 46:10)

  and

  Be still and know that I am human and don't have to play God anymore.

- I am thankful for the dreams, even the disconcerting ones, of last night as well as the ones I will be having today, while awake.

We do not seek to see ourselves in running water, but in still water. For only what is itself still can impart stillness in others.

Chuang-Tse

Be still and acknowledge that I don't own anything, including my soul; I merely inhabit it.
Be still and allow the hidden, unconscious streams to flow.
Be still and allow the whisperings of conscience to stir and

the fountain of tears to pour forth.

Be still and allow clarity to come to the muddy pool as well as the confused spirit.

I say "allow" because we can never produce, garner, or win "the grace of being still." We can only invite or thwart its presence.

Motionless statues

Health requires this relaxation, this aimless life. This life in the present.

Thoreau

On my early morning walk I hear a hawk flying overhead. I look skyward, and as my glance gradually descends to earth, I spot two exquisite fawns 100 yards up a nearby slope. Camouflaged and still, yet perceptible.

What marvelously agile animals—darting one moment, stationary the next—capable of shifting from rapid speed to motionlessness, in fractions of seconds. The deer know I am watching them. I pause in awe, then keep sauntering. I return half an hour later, and they are yet still.

Shady, my walking companion, lunges into the bushes after a rabbit, and my head spins with her. Then I quickly look back up the hill.

The fawns are gone. Fully present elsewhere.

The void shows through

God made everything out of nothing, but the nothingness
shows through.

Paul Valéry

When I am alone, silent, and still, I am apt to experience the
void. As a product of Western culture, I fear formlessness. "Nothing" intimidates me. I furiously fill my tranquil moments and
empty spaces. Yet mindful of Zen Buddhist wisdom, I am starting
to conceive of the void not as a chaotic pit or cosmic blank but as
a dynamic container, akin to my Tibetan singing bowl, where
absence furnishes the context for elegant shape and sacred sound.
Trappist monk Thomas Merton calls this telling intersection of
silence, solitude, and stillness—"the virginal point of pure nothingness which is at the center of all other loves."

Could it be?

I spend the remainder of my day sparring with Merton's
mystifying claim.

"Grow slowly to last long"

It is with us as with trees; we must grow slowly to last long.

Thoreau

Two of the most common words in Thoreau's *Walden* lexicon are "desperate" and "deliberate."

Desperate. "Why should we be in such desperate haste to succeed and in such desperate enterprises?" he writes and then later: " . . . most people lead lives of quiet desperation . . . " As a descriptor, "desperate" vividly depicts late-20th-century Americans. We are addicted to leading harried, hassled, hurried, and, therewith, hobbled lives. Our desperation isn't even quiet.

The unswerving foe of "desperate" is "deliberate":

I went to the woods because I wished to live deliberately, to front only the essential facts of life, and see if I could learn what it had to teach, and not, when I came to die, discover that I had not lived.

Thoreau employs "deliberate" repeatedly to remind "desperate" individuals that we are not helpless to alter the pace of our lives. Let each of us pay attention to the "different drummer" in our hearts. "Let us step to the music that we hear, however measured or far away." Let us select a velocity of life that expands rather than shrinks our souls, that saves "but a tiny core of stillness in the heart like the eye of a violet" (D.H. Lawrence).

One of "the essential facts of life" is that without stillness our psyches languish. However, stillness won't miraculously fall into our laps. We must deliberately create the conditions under which moments of tranquility and calm can flourish. Here at Dorland I practice "slow-down" arts like: *blushing* or displaying reverent modesty around the foliage, fauna, and four-legged friends in the woods; *brooding* or sitting pensively as creations are hatched within and about me; *dawdling* or loitering without purpose; and *hovering* or fluttering about, suspended in the air.

Yet such deliberateness poses a ticklish problem for, if we aren't careful, we can burden ourselves with well-intentioned yet contradictory injunctions like: "Come on now, soul, be still and produce for me!" This is why the ancient Tibetan advice comes in handy, "Friend, hasten slowly, hasten slowly!" Or as Thoreau wrote: "It is with us as with trees; we must grow slowly to last long."

Sleeping in the forest

I thought the earth remembered me, she took me back so
tenderly, arranging her dark skirts, her pockets full of li-
chens and seeds. I slept as never before, a stone on the
riverbed, nothing between me and the white fire of the
stars but my thoughts, and they floated light as moths among
the branches of the perfect trees. All night I rose and fell,
as if in water, grappling with a luminous doom. By morning I had vanished at least a dozen times into something
better.

Mary Oliver

Thoreau was something of a daytime devotee. His moral
imagery invariably favored morning and light:

To those whose elastic and vigorous thought keeps pace
with the sun, the day is a perpetual morning. It matters not
what the clocks say or the attitudes and labors of people.
Morning is when I am awake and there is a dawn in me.
Moral reform is the effort to throw off sleep.

On the contrary, I would sing praises to my sleep, however
erratic, and the learnings therein, for I believe what Job says:
"God gives us songs in our sleep." They may be strange, trou-
bling songs sometimes, but melodies nonetheless. Indeed, monks

are never averse to new initiates sleeping all the time they are on retreat, because that may be exactly what they need.

Tucked inside my lightly insulated mountain cabin, I might as well be sleeping in the forest. Noises of the night rake my nerves, because there is so little protection between me and the outdoors. I sleep unevenly, churning over both angels and beasts in my sleep. In my dreams I run to embrace dead friends and am chased by live enemies. Plants greet me, and animals dance with me. My head swims with a multitude of mundanities.

My nights are still, yet seldom without turbulence.

Sleeping in the forest is no less integral to my sojourn than periods of sauntering, meditation, writing. Paradoxically, the dark and chill of nighttime disturb *and* settle me. I doubt if I will ever resolve my conflicted feelings of both fright and comfort in the arms of night.

Poet Robert Bly notes that "performance escapes soul," especially for high achievers such as artists, ministers, business leaders, and teachers. The better we perform, the less our soul shows. During the daylight I am performing continuously, in one fashion or another. When I climb under the covers, the stagelights go off, the curtain slams shut, the play is over, the applause fades. I stop performing, at least to familiar audiences.

Yet the poet Saint-Pol-Roux reminds us that we labor even in our dreams. He used to hang the inscription, "The poet working," from his door before going to sleep.

And so it goes. My soul grows in awkward yet measurable bursts as I slumber in the forest.

Being

When we would rest our bodies, we cease to support them;
we recline on the lap of earth. So, when we would rest our
spirits, we must recline on the Great Spirit. Let things alone;
let them weigh what they will; let them soar or fall.

Thoreau

Thoreau was not interested in doing good works in order to
receive entrance into eternal life. His aim was to be a good person, holy and awake, while walking this earth. He was focused
not on *doing* but on *being*–what the Tao Te Ching named *wu-wei*
or "creative quietude." "I honor you," wrote Thoreau's friend
Harrison Gray Otis Blake, "because you abstain from action, and
open your soul that you may be somewhat."

Conversely, it takes me more effort to be someone than to do
something. I need to draw a deep breath, quit trying so hard,
surrender, be still . . . be. I think of hibernating animals, passing
the winter in a torpid state. This February is my hibernation of
soul, an opening to be dormant.

On my walk today, I halt in amazement at the placid hills.
Nothing moves. Nature's stillness summons my own. Lao Tzu
observed that, as in nature, the tree that bends with the winds
survives, and the water that yields to the rock in its path eventu-
ally wears the hard stone down. Wise persons heed Lao Tsu's
advice: "to yield is to be preserved whole."

So I exercise my embryonic knack of sitting still outdoors. Amid a grove of trees, I lounge upon a large boulder and observe a murmuring stream cascading gently over a profusion of rocks. This is no raging river but a faithfully flowing stream which has smoothed many a stone over the centuries.

Likewise my soul smoothes out some during this sabbath. The Zen master Dogen, after a lengthy stay alone in the woods, was asked: "What did you learn?" He leisurely yet confidently replied: "Softness of heart, softness of heart." I wholeheartedly concur.

My heart will return to the metropolis from the mountain with manifold rough spots and ruts leveled.

"Sound of a gentle stillness"

> . . . but the Lord was not in the fire; and after the fire, a still small voice . . .
>
> I Kings 19:12

The accurate translation of this famous theophany, "a still small voice," is "sound of a gentle stillness." Either version is instructive for us forest-dwellers.

The days that follow Elijah's triumph over hundreds of Baal priests are depressing ones. The public cheering quickly leaves Elijah and turns to follow his enemy, Queen Jezebel. Elijah feels deserted by God as well.

Despondent and anxious, he heads into the wilderness. He is willing to die, "it is enough, now, take away my life; for I am no better than my fathers." Then Elijah flees to a cave and lodges there. Grousing in self-pity, Elijah hears the various sounds of earthquake, wind, and fire, but God's voice dwells in none of them. Then he hears the "sound of a gentle stillness" imploring him, "What are you doing here, Elijah?"

As with Adam and Eve in the Garden of Eden, God's question poses a concern of spiritual not physical geography. "What are you doing here, Elijah?" In other words, what is your purpose in life now? What remains for you to do, Elijah? He balks, then God probes a second time, more strongly, following this question with a command for Elijah to go back home, anoint another religious leader to take his place, then retire and rest in peace. Which is what comes to pass.

Elijah went to the woods to hide away from God and humanity, collect his thoughts, and nurse his wounds. I went to the woods for different reasons, to make inroads into soul and nature. God's piercing call reaches us via the "sound of a gentle stillness," a sound both baffling and energizing, yet insistently real.

Chapter IV

Simplicity

"Simplicity, simplicity, simplicity"

> Simplicity, simplicity, simplicity! I can say, let your affairs
> be as two or three, and not a hundred or a thousand; in-
> stead of a million count half a dozen, and keep your ac-
> counts on your thumbnail.
>
> Thoreau

This is one of Thoreau's enduring refrains. He not only re-
peats the word "simplicity" three times, but later, in the same
section, utters the imperative: "Simplify, simplify!"

It is easy to romanticize Thoreau's sojourn at Walden Pond,
forgetting that his was a more carefree existence than most. He
was without partner or children, used rent-free space from the
Emersons to build his cabin, and walked regularly back to Concord to enjoy his friend's company and his mother's vittles. Nonetheless, Thoreau practiced an essential existence. He abided by
"higher laws" that enabled him to focus not on livelihood so much
as on life itself. His embodiment of the simple life remains extra-
ordinarily relevant today.

The two basic regions of exploration for Thoreau at Walden
and for me at Dorland are nature and soul—the interplay between
and the depths within each. Such a basic, focused mission has
furnished abundant material to satisfy my entire mind and month.

Once, when asked at the dinner table which dish he preferred,
Thoreau answered in typical fashion: "The nearest." Likewise,

when I am outdoors in the woods, I dwell on what is nearest to me in the natural world amidst its subtle and profligate splendor. When I am inside Orchard House, I attend to my soul and explore its innermost territories through chanting, sitting still, reflection, writing, and even sleep.

So, my adventure at Dorland has proven inordinately simple, yet as Thoreau cautions fellow forest-dwellers, "Philosopher's simplicity: outwardly simple; inwardly complex."

A wood-shed will suffice

The youth gets together materials to build a bridge to the moon or perchance a palace or temple on the earth, and at length the middle-aged person concludes to build a wood-shed with them.

Thoreau

Thoreau and I both find it difficult to identify with the dreams of palatial proportions advanced by exuberant youth. In Hindu parlance, "forest-dwellers" have little in common with either "students" or "householders."

The afternoon aspirations of mid-life are simple: a wood-shed to house some garden tools with which to putter around in the yard. In this case, my particular wood-shed project is as expansive as the entire outdoors and as fathomless as my very soul.

My friends were curious when they heard Dorland had no electricity. What would any reputable, efficient writer do without a computer? Since I tend to be a technological Neanderthal, I rejoice in being encumbered with no more writing arsenal than my yellow pad, a dozen pencils and sharpener, scotch tape, scissors, paper clips, and Webster's New Collegiate Dictionary.

While they flood my mind, let me pay allegiance to other inanimate treasures that suffuse Orchard House, objects with which I grow a strange yet abiding affection: my green Coleman lantern, the yellow-coated vegetable pot, my favorite (one and only) stubby glass, the ceramic roasted almond holder (which I seldom use but often admire), the bright poster of a red type-writer by Anne Laddon wittily entitled, "Red Writer," the delicate stained-glass window depicting three flowering bulbs, the eccentric floor-length mirror in the bedroom, my dependable fire-preparation and clean-up tools, the cracked windows, the slanted tin soap container in the shower. These are but a few of my favorite things at Orchard House.

Most of my Dorland ink is understandably spilled over the animals, chaparral, the paths and vistas, my soul-stretching explorations. Yet with the spare effects I brought to the woods and the munificence I have discovered while dwelling here, I feel blessed with abundant wealth.

Shedding

Perhaps middle age is, or should be, a period of shedding shells; the shell of ambition, the shell of material accumulations and possessions, the shell of the ego. Perhaps one can shed at this stage in life as one sheds in beach-living; one's pride, one's false ambitions, one's mask, one's armor . . . and what a liberation that would be!

Anne Morrow Lindbergh

We are rich in proportion to the number of things which we can afford to let alone.

Thoreau

When we lived in Davenport, Iowa, one of the big church events both Fall and Spring was the rummage sale. The entire downstairs of our compact church building was inundated with priceless "junk." During those weekends, children, youth, and adults crammed upstairs into our sanctuary for worship because there was literally no room below except for salespeople, customers, bodyguards, and the aforementioned stuff.

We even built an additional room on the premises to house the appurtenances necessary for storing and setting up yet the next rummage. Since it was constructed during my ministerial regime, they whimsically named it "The Tom Owen-Towle Shed."

I don't exaggerate when I say that rummage sales were rites of passage equal in stature to Christmas and Easter on our liturgical calendar.

In retrospect, more was happening than making dollars and unloading worthless stuff. Rummage weekends were religious reminders for us to take unfailing inventory of our lives, to sort out the miscellany of our existence: weighing what was essential to keep and what could be discarded, forcing us ravenous Westerners to discriminate between greed and need.

I was converted. I now host periodic garage sales, clean out my files and bookcases annually, even give away clothes and artifacts to admirers, sometimes right on the spot. You may judge me compulsive, but I travel more jauntily when my environment is stripped of clutter. As the song goes: "'Tis a gift to be simple, 'tis a gift to be free, 'tis a gift to come down where we ought to be." My freedom in life results largely from simplifying my existence.

I call this the art of shedding; it falls under Thoreau's rubric of "simplicity." The older I get, the clearer I become about what I can and can't do, what I will and won't relinquish. Focus and shed, focus and shed, focus and shed until I am paring my life down to basics.

Interestingly, the more I shed physical relics, the more energy I conserve to salute a fascinating panoply of persons such as ancestors, mentors, gods and goddesses, friends, foes, famous figures known only indirectly, and fictitious characters.

This February, residing in the Temecula Valley, I am inspired to honor some of my predecessors who have passed this way, being shaped by and shaping this gorgeous parcel of golden land: Kit Carson, Juan Murrieta, L. Canpasahpish, Helen Hunt Jackson, Pio Pico, and all the nameless Native Americans, conquistadores, padres, trappers, argonauts, and, yes, the countless thieves.

When we arrive at life's conclusion, we will not be asked

how many items did we accumulate or how many meetings did we attend, but rather how deeply did we give ourselves to the values and beings we cherished. I'm trying to get ready now.

In my wallet rests a maxim from the poet e.e. cummings: "Love is the every only God who sang this earth so glad and big." My prevailing purpose in life is to love in response to the love that sang this earth so glad and big.

I love best after shedding.

Unadorned psalms

Haiku's spare frolic
Crisp, condensed explorations
No excess baggage

Horribly despoiled
Litter, litter everywhere
Unholy legacy

Above, during night
Wind tenderly raking roof
Inscrutable calm

Morning walk palette
Greens twisting, hoary lilacs
Beige, reddish-orange streaks

Hoarse frogs in chorus
Swift-winged, low-murmuring doves
Wild delicacies

Rain leaking through planks
Directly upon the bed
Torture not my aim

Ticanu, my pond?
Nature's offspring, unpossessed
Only to ponder

Wintu Indians:
"Wherever White Man touches
    earth,
It is sore, very sore."

Unwelcome night-guests
Create veritable zoo
Vermin on the loose

Tunes from all quarters
Nature's antiphonal choir
Silence is broken

Trees talk steadily
Humans turn away, ears plugged
Precious fables lost

Inside soul's chamber
Dark streams, cascading canyons
Grazing homegrown herbs

Born, grew in Concord
Traveled some outside Concord
Buried in Concord

Some essentials

In an ultimate sense I cannot know what I do in this place, yet I do ultimate things. Essentially I cannot know what I do, yet I do essential things.

Peter Shafer

I went to the woods because I wished to live deliberately, to front only the essential facts of life . . .

Thoreau

Dorland and Thoreau have forced me to prune, then prune some more, my essentials to a nourishing few—essentials sturdy yet elastic enough to transport my soul far, far into tomorrows beyond counting.

First, I choose to experience some beauty, inner and outer, every day so if I should suddenly die, it would be enough.

Second, as Thoreau urges, "I must live above all in the present." This means, I plan for the future, I remember my pasts, but I dwell only in the present.

Third, Thoreau penned in another Journal entry that "you must walk so gently as to hear the finest sounds, the faculties being in repose. Your mind must not perspire." One of Dorland's chief lessons has been to slow down, sit still, sleep, saunter—don't sweat life, large or small stuff, so much. I am practicing the fundamental "four dignities" recommended by the Chinese: "Standing, lying, sitting, and walking."

Fourth, Emerson, with gentle yet sustained fury, criticized his friend Thoreau's lack of ambition:

> I so much regret the loss of his rare power of action, that I cannot help counting it a fault in him that he had no ambition. Wanting this instead of engineering for all America, he was the captain of a huckleberry party. Pounding beans is good to the end of pounding empires one of these days; but if at the end of years, it is still only beans!

Yet Thoreau wasn't about to measure up to an externally imposed standard of excellence, even one set by his mentor, Emerson. He was who he was–a solitary character, loyal to his espoused assignments as "a mystic, transcendentalist, prophet."

The irony is that Emerson would have been pleasantly startled by the cluster of persons who saluted Thoreau's exemplary life long after both of them were gone. Thoreau's legacy has been revered through quote and deed by a wide range of distinguished individuals: Mahatma Gandhi, Loren Eiseley, Emma Goldman, Sinclair Lewis, Robert Lowell, Ernest Hemingway, John F. Kennedy, Edwin Way Teale, Lord Tweedsmuir, Gene Tunney, Martin Luther King, Jr., Malcolm X, George Bernard Shaw, Robert Frost, and Franklin Delano Roosevelt.

Finally, the measuring rod of any sojourn into the woods, such as Thoreau's, is whether its lessons are embodied during one's homestretch. Thoreau left Walden Pond after 26 months, but the remaining 14 years of his short life exhibit the same ferocious devotion to simplicity, journal writing, and excursions into soul and nature that he had initiated at Walden Pond. He even continued his pattern of committing mornings to writing, afternoons to observing nature, and evenings to books and company.

I will have more difficulty than Thoreau in replicating Dorland back home in San Diego, but my soul-journey, if of enduring worth, will modify appreciably the focus and pace of my remaining years. I am dedicated to lengthening my experiments at Ticanu Pond in being inwardly rich and outwardly simple.

Chapter V

Darkness

"A very different season"

Many walk by day; few walk by night. It is a very different season.

Thoreau

At Dorland I usually walk morning, noon, and night. Each time unveils a distinct universe. In the morning time, there is considerable frost in the air, and the sun is barely climbing into view. I plunge into the chaparral of the countryside, forging my way through its thicket of dense shrubs and evergreen oaks.

In the afternoon, I walk because I am weary of mining thoughts and scrawling notes. I covet a physical interlude.

In the early evening, as darkness arrives, I walk for a different reason. I walk primarily to befriend an old foe. Ever since I can remember, I have been uneasy in the dark. It gets pitch dark at Ticanu Pond.

As a child I always slept with the hall light on or the shades slightly pulled. I would call out to my mother, in the foreboding darkness, to gain my bearings and insure my safety. At Dorland I sleep with two flashlights nearby, one on the night-stand, the other loosely gripped in my hand, ready for rapid use.

If truth be told, I am both repelled by and attracted to darkness. As a youngster, walking home alone from my friend's house several blocks away, I would defy the dark to scare me, if it could; to swallow me, if it might.

Even as an adult, I will enter, after dark, the heart of forbidden zones—downtowns or unsafe parks—race in and out, always on the fly. I perform these feats, mind you, with my running shoes laced. I deem this weird behavior my continuing way of daring the demons of the dark. Flirting with some of the real and imaginary terrors in the outside world seemingly forearms me for wrangling with the fears roaming inside my psyche.

"A little afraid of the dark"

> I believe that people are generally still a little afraid of the dark though the witches are all hung, and Christianity and candles have been introduced.
>
> Thoreau

Today we are just as frightened of the dark as in 1845, maybe more so. As a matter of fact, the witches aren't all hung; people continue to be destroyed cruelly in every land for irrational reasons. World religions, including Christianity, while irradiating considerable light, also perpetrate dastardly deeds in the name of divine sanction.

My candles, kerosene and Coleman lanterns, while helpful, will never banish the darkness inside and outside my soul. I resonate with Ruth Gendler's balanced assessment:

> The dictionary defines "night" in terms of day and "day" in terms of night. Can we find a way to talk about light and dark without talking about good and bad? To love both day and night? Can we hold the beauty of both in the same breath?

Truly, it is written in Genesis: "There was evening, and there was morning, one day." Each 24-hour sweep is unified, of a whole. Light and dark, day and night are merely different seasons, creating together the terrifyingly beautiful reality we designate as life. Darkness includes manifold positives and negatives on its continuum. So does light. There are dark moments that nourish us enormously; let us salute them. There are dark acts that reveal our malevolent nature; let us dispel them.

To remain "a little afraid of the dark" is understandable.

"To know the dark"

To go in the dark with a light is to know the light. To know the dark, go dark. Go without sight, and find that the dark, too, blooms and sings, and is traveled by dark feet and dark wings.

Wendell Berry

Darkness comes earlier than usual to Orchard House tonight. I have eaten my evening meal and instead of lighting all my lanterns, I astound myself by choosing to acquiesce to the mounting dark.

I chant and sing. The coals of the fire are but embers now.

I ring my singing bowl and chew over the day gone by.

I shake my rattle and blithely mouth whatever sentiments ache to be heard. The darkness thickens.

I sit quietly, then motionless, in my "solitude" chair and slip into the dark, deep, deep, deeper into the dark, mindful of the dark, warm room of my mother's body, where my life began—safe, unassailable, wanted.

I await the unguarded sounds of nature and uncensored sensations of soul circulating in the hours ahead. For the conversations I have with myself in pitch dark are markedly different from my daytime dialogues.

"We work in the dark."

We work in the dark. We do what we can. We give what we have. Our doubt is our passion. Our passion is our task. The rest is the madness of art.

Henry James

I find it hard to conceive of the endarkened setting of my wilderness cohorts, Sam and Billie Wright. They dwelt from 1968 to 1988 in an arctic clime where there was no direct sunlight for three months at a time. How did they endure?

True creativity is sometimes spurred by the absence of normal "creature comforts." Without reassuring sunshine, "we work in the dark" and "do what we can" with who we are now, not yesterday or tomorrow, and the imaginative urge sustains itself.

We write to survive. We write to put dragons to rest and set angels to dancing. We write because we must. It remains the holiest way to send order or chaos, or both, coursing through our veins.

I envision Annie Dillard writing from her "pine shed on Cape Cod . . . eight feet by ten feet." She sobers all creative ones by declaring:

Appealing workplaces are to be avoided. One wants a room with no view, so imagination can meet memory in the dark.

Staring at the fireplace furnishes heat but, more significantly, throws me back upon myself, keeps me inwardly focused, right where I belong. My imagination and memory are beginning to covet whatever moments they can steal together in the dark.

Dark nights of the soul

We die of cold and not of darkness.

Miguel de Unamuno

Medieval mystics like Hildegard of Bingen and John of the Cross labeled their times of spiritual aridity and torment: "dark nights of the soul." Mechtild of Magdeburg describes her period of religious anguish as follows:

> There comes a time when both body and soul enter into such a vast darkness that one loses light and consciousness and knows nothing more of God's intimacy. At such a time when the light in the lantern burns out, the beauty of the lantern can no longer be seen. With longing and distress we are reminded of our nothingness.

During the bleak stretches lining our soul-journeys, we pilgrims feel God's absence and our own emptiness. Yet we have been known to re-emerge from such hollows as more resilient and expansive beings. Encouraged by the testimonies of Hildegard, John, Mechtild, and countless other spiritual voyagers, I navigate, ever so carefully, my own descent into darkness to be purified without mortification.

They say, and I am beginning to trust, that no one, no one dies of the dark.

"I have faith in nights"

You darkness, that I come from, I love you more than all the
fires that fence in the world, for the fire makes a circle of
light for everyone, and then no one outside learns of you.
But the darkness pulls in everything: shapes and fire, animals and myself, how easily it gathers them!—powers and
people—and it is possible a great energy is moving near
me. I have faith in nights.

Rainer Maria Rilke

Probably my toughest assignment at Dorland is to grow friendlier with the night, pure darkness unsoftened by lights, programs,
warm bodies. I desire, along with my favorite German poet, Rilke,
to "have faith in nights." Elsewhere, Rilke even equates divinity
with darkness: "No matter how deeply I go down into myself my
God is dark, and like a webbing made of a hundred roots, that
drink in silence."

Thoreau was also a creature of the day, especially the morning. He would take night walks, to be sure, and found them
"medicative and fertilizing" (an intriguing pair of modifiers), but
he was never comfortable with the night as a physical reality or
spiritual metaphor. As Robert Richardson notes:

Indeed the whole subject of night has, for Thoreau, sinister,
tragic, misanthropic potential. Talking of night as the "mere

negation of day," he added, "Death is with me and life far away." He found it ominous that, as we grow older, "we have more to say about evening, less about morning."

Here in the wintry woods, I don layers of bulk to cushion my skeleton against the snappy air seeping through the wooden planks. Perhaps I also cover my body, and therewith armor my soul, to counter the premonitions and intruders of darkness, commuting at large, all night long.

Tonight, I modify my course. I cautiously wonder: "Dare I permit my anxious, moist being to mingle with the murky dark rather than hiding from it? Why suit up as if for a battle? After all, is not my sojourn about mustering sufficient bravery rather than deadening my soul in cowardice?" Neither in a futile quest to banish the darkness, as Western religions are wont to do, nor willing to embrace it, as some practitioners of black magic or satanism exhort, I am satisfied with encountering darkness in friendlier fashion.

The older I grow, the more I seek to explore the night, to court it as in a dance, and to weave my way toward some peaceful existence, perhaps a satisfying grasp. So, with ample shyness, I gingerly unwrap portions of my body and soul to the presence of the engulfing darkness. And I softly vocalize in chant-like measure, the comforting refrain of Papago, the owl woman: "In the great night my heart will go out, toward me the darkness comes rattling. In the great night my heart will go out."

Curse of darkness

In our culture, white is esteemed, it is "superior," associated with such states as heavenly, sun-like, clean, pure, immaculate, innocent, and beautiful. At the same time, our language portrays a generally negative usage of the word black, associating it with sin, evil, wicked, gloomy, depressing, angry, sullen. Ascribing negative and positive values, respectively, to colors black and white enhances the institutionalization of this country's racist values.

Jacqui James

My colleague's depiction, however painful to admit, lodges on target. When pre-teen black children were asked to choose which black or white boys and girls were more beautiful and likely to be smarter, better-behaved kids, the black children lamentably chose the "white ones." They have been indoctrinated by the prevailing currents in American society.

Despite respecting the life-patterns of Native Americans, Thoreau still reflects the pervasive racial bias of his era when he wrote in October 1852:

The constitution of the Indian mind appears to be the very opposite to that of the white man. He is acquainted with a different side of nature. He measures his life by winters, not summers. His year is not measured by the sun, but consists of a certain number of moons, and his moons are not measured by days, but by nights. He has taken hold of the dark side of nature, the white man, the bright side.

Sounds similar to our cultural stigma attached to the darker races today, doesn't it?

In the early 1900s black activist W. E. DuBois declared that color would furnish America with its most contentious issue of the 20th century. We have proven him correct, not only on this continent, but around the globe.

Regardless of racial progress, despite numerous instances of respect and even affection conveyed across lines of color, as this century winds down, we white males still inhabit positions of unwarranted privilege and are rarely willing to redistribute resources equitably or relinquish power readily. Truth-telling with persons of color, while crucial, is insufficient work. Racism is predominantly a white problem. I must be courageous enough to speak truth to the powers that be in my own race. To assault institutional racism entails battling the normative culture in our modern world.

I remember my father sharing his feelings of inferiority on merely being the "darker" of the two Towle boys. His mother, Clorinda Ramirez, of direct Hispanic lineage, secretly preferred his lighter-skinned brother Wilber over my father. At school Harold was the butt of racial slurs. He never quite shook loose his ingrained sense of inferiority. A modest and isolated yet telling casualty of racism.

There is no easy road to freedom as Nelson Mandela, black South African activist, laments. There is no easy road to dismantling institutional racism, but I have learned, back home as well as in the woods, truths that impel myself and society toward greater racial sensitivity.

To march and confess, study and protest keeps us focused, alert, and laboring on this recalcitrant problem. Such involvement, however partial and flawed, enables us to organize rather than simply agonize over racism, to gnaw at the roots and symptoms of this pervasive injustice. It keeps us honest. It keeps us morally sane.

We are always but one gesture, one person away from intensifying racism. We need a critically supportive community to monitor our attitudes and behaviors. We need courageous allies of diverse colors alongside us in the relentless push for equality.

Dealing with my deeply imbedded, twin fears of dark sky and dark skin keeps me active on both personal and social fronts. Our internal anxieties and external prejudices are often subtly yet inextricably bound together.

I am a recovering racist and will be engaged in such moral combat for the rest of my life, so I can place humble breakthroughs and disappointing setbacks in a long-haul context. As the glorious spiritual exhorts: "I know one thing we did right was the day we started to fight. Keep your eyes on the prize, hold on, hold on."

We concluded our Martin Luther King, Jr. Sunday worship service recently by joining hands and singing together, "We Shall Overcome." The black sky and white sun merged at this propitious moment and gave birth to a cloudburst of showers, long overdue in our parched Southern California desert. Our gathered congregation of various colors was symbolically cleansed in this downpour, and, if but for a while, bound closer together in anguish and in hope.

"Treasures of darkness"

I will give you the treasures of darkness and the hoards
from my secret places.

Isaiah 45:3

Truth strikes us from behind, and in the dark, as well as
from before and in broad daylight.

Thoreau

My uneasy yet accelerating truce with the darkness within
my soul and amid my environs has spawned fresh appreciation.
I am cognizant of and increasingly thankful that things grow in
the dark. As Thoreau acknowledges: "I believe in the forest, and
in the meadow, and in the night in which the corn grows."

Yet much more than corn develops in the dark. Dreams
emerge in the dark. Our earth came into being when darkness
brooded upon the face of the deep. Indeed, humus, from which
our germinal concepts of humor, humanness, human, and humility all sprout, refers to the dark, organic portion of soil. We
evolve from the darkness of our mother's wombs. And what about
stars–those natural, luminous, celestial wonders? They covet the
dark in order to exhibit their radiant glory. And who of us lovers
doesn't concur with poet Marge Piercy's depiction that "love is

plunging into darkness toward a place that may exist"? And God? Well, it was Meister Eckhart who contended, "God is superessential darkness." These words countervail our Western bias that describes divinity primarily in terms of enlightenment.

It is interesting to note that according to Jewish calendars the day begins at sundown and not at sunup. Furthermore, all festivals and holy days start at night–to test our faith, I imagine.

We humans grow, most profoundly, when we affirm the shadow side of our character, meet head on our inner demons, and endure the inexplicable sorrows that befall us.

I am an upbeat and sunshiny person (raised amidst the Southern California rays) who has tried to transcend, rather than transform, the agonies of life. Whenever I can circumvent pain, I try to do so. But my love affair with sunshine has caught up with me. I suffer from recurring skin cancer, having almost lost sight in my right eye. My dermatologist continues to burn and dig away at my flesh, as I keep paying for genetic susceptibility and willful overexposure, especially as a youth.

> If there are any who think that I am vainglorious, that I set myself above others and crow over their low estate, let me tell them that I could tell a pitiful story respecting myself as well as them...I could encourage them with a sufficient list of failures, and could flow as humbly as the very gutters.
>
> Thoreau

My own moral ugliness has run me down as well. I can no longer avoid facing the results of my hurtful behavior in life– most scathingly, the virtual abandonment of my youngest child as I melded a new family 2000 miles away. While our bond has been restored, the searing hurt and damage remain.

There is more. I am not the dove I espouse; hawks soar in my cavernous being and feast at my table. I am not the "golden boy" of my dreams and early press reviews. My days of vainglory are finished. My life, like Thoreau's, constitutes "a sufficient list of failures."

The truth is I am outgrowing what Robert Bly called, in reference to his own evolution, "the maddening cheerfulness" of my earlier years. In so doing, I am migrating toward greater selfhood, toward inclusion of my various parts—good and bad, beautiful and ugly. My innocence has been shattered late but permanently. The good little *boy* is sluggishly evolving into a checkered, yet fuller *man*.

Thoreau again:

> There is a certain fertile sadness which I would not avoid, but rather earnestly seek. It is positively joyful to me. It saves my life from being trivial.

I am reclaiming the sad as well as the offensive features of my odyssey, and it likewise "saves my life from being trivial." The primary cutting edge of adult male psycho-spiritual growth is admission of loss. The proper attitude for men to hold in the face of our wounding and being wounded is sorrow not blame, yet due to rigid socialization, our preferred attitudes tend to be denial and retaliation toward women as well as toward children and other men.

When I am forthright, I can personally recount a sufficient list of both hurts and guilts. I do not number myself among the gravely wounded, but my soul contains abundant sadness, and only as I bravely descend into my ashes am I regenerated and lifted to holier ground. I concur with James Hillman, who, referring to Hans Castorp in Thomas Mann's *The Magic Mountain* and the spot of tuberculosis on Castorp's lung, says, "Through the little hole of his wound, the immense realm of the spirit enters."

"Blessed are those who mourn," says the New Testament, "for

they shall be comforted," and, I would add, they shall grow as well. I used to avoid grieving by retreating to my cheerful disguise. I now trust grieving to be a sign of spiritual vitality. I used to equate sadness with dolefulness. I know better now. Being woundable and feeling sad come with the territory of being fully awake. Sad people aren't desperate; while acknowledging the thorns, they keep mulching rose gardens.

Shepherd Bliss shares sound doctrine on this matter when he writes:

> The Dalai Lama has pointed out that his monks tend to go up into spirit rather than down into soul. You see, spirit rises and soul is in the valley—and they were up in the Himalayas. . . . We all know about the peak experience that you get from chanting, but often it's the soul, the sadness, the grief, the going down into the valleys that allows you to grow up into ecstasy.

At Dorland, the tears come easily, for as someone commented, "tears flow at those moments when we do." I am flowing in the woods; my melancholy abounds without being mawkish.

Thoreau, for all his seeming composure and self-sufficiency, was wracked with inner pain. Wanting to eternalize his innocence, he wept when his mother finally told him to leave home and make his way in the world. Then his beloved older brother, John, died from a freakish shaving accident in his early twenties.

John was nursed daily by Henry and finally died in his arms. Henry was distraught and fell ill with sympathetic lockjaw. He ceased writing in his life-blood journal for nearly two months while recovering himself. Henry could never talk about John thereafter without tears welling up.

A few short years after his brother's death, Thoreau withdrew from society and entered the woods, in part, to do some writing in his beloved brother's memory.

Thoreau was never able to sustain an erotic bond, and even his best friendship—with Ralph Waldo Emerson—was strained by reciprocal hurts. And I have always found Thoreau's eyes hauntingly mournful. In a poetic fragment he mused: "Greater is the depth of sadness than is any height of gladness." His life disclosed that truth.

Matters of the soul have to do ultimately, according to Jungian therapists, medieval mystics, and Thoreau, with descent not ascent, vulnerability not stoicism, plumbing the moist, dusky regions of the dark humus.

Chapter VI

Sensuousness

Morning prayer

Ohiyesa, the Santee Dakota physician and author, wrote in 1911 about the manner in which his people worship:

> In the life of the Indian there was only one inevitable duty—the duty of prayer—the daily recognition of the Unseen and Eternal. Daily devotions were more necessary than daily food. . . . Each soul must meet the morning sun, the new sweet earth and the Great Silence alone!

So this morning, standing tall before the advancing dawn and facing the sun, I bow in prayer:

> Great Silence,
> Thank you for another day—
> A blessing beyond my deserving,
> Full of happy and sad gifts beyond my expectation.
> Open my eyes that I might see,
> Open my ears that I might hear,
> Open my nostrils that I might smell,
> Open my mouth that I might taste,
> Open my hands that I might touch,
> Open my soul that I might entertain
>   marvels exceeding comprehension and
>   mysteries eluding capture.
> Peace and unrest, unrest and peace. Amen.

"Employ your senses"

We live but a fraction of our life. Why do we not let on the flood, raise the gates, and set all our wheels in motion? Those who hath ears, let them hear. Employ your senses.

Thoreau

Henry David Thoreau cultivated "a purely sensuous life." Elsewhere he remarked: "My body is all sentient." He savored pleasure through gratification of the senses. For him, beauty wasn't merely in the eyes of the beholder; it permeated one's entire being.

During his afternoon excursions, Thoreau would whet all his senses: the sound of birds, the sight of the sun, the taste of wild berries, the smell of flowers, the feel of the marsh. "We can never have enough of nature," he rhapsodized.

Consequently, you would find Thoreau standing in the swamp "up to his chin," drenching his body in the opulent "juices" of the bog, yet keeping his head, the reflective organ, above it all. This way, his instinctive and intellectual natures were equally stimulated.

Thoreau was not a sensually indulgent person deficient in moral pursuits. Hardly. For Thoreau, employing one's senses was unquestionably a spiritual discipline. In experiencing nature up close, he encountered the holy, the transcendent, God directly.

Thoreau waxed mystical about his sensuous activities. He

referred to hearing "beyond the range of sound" and seeing "beyond the verge of sight." He went so far as to say that he could "see, smell, taste . . . feel that everlasting Something." God, he felt, could be apprehended by "divine germs called the senses." For Thoreau, the fully sensuous and wholly spiritual person were one and the same.

Thoreau was a naturalistic philosopher, an ecological mystic—a zany, incorrigible blend. I am an embryonic naturalist, but I don't come by this persuasion easily. I didn't complete Boy Scout training. I have usually camped in the woods, believing that time spent in nature would prove "worthwhile" for me. I have also been prone to display the arrogant habit of anthropomorphizing the natural world—translating animals, plants, stones, and oceans in human terms.

Nonetheless, Dorland is pushing me to profounder, more equitable levels of kinship with nature. I am climbing out of my "head" and coming more to my "senses," and therewith, enlarging my soul in unanticipated, wondrous ways.

We live in an urbanized culture where music tapes that capture wilderness sounds are sold at "nature" retail stores, so that the woods can effortlessly infiltrate our suburban homes. At Dorland I am experiencing the woods more naturally. I am partaking of a sumptuous, sensory stew.

O hospitable ones!

I was a stranger and you took me in.

Gospel of Matthew

What would the world be, once bereft of wet and of wilderness? Let them be left, O let them be left, wildness and wet; Long live the weeds and the wilderness yet.

Gerard Manley Hopkins

Raptors, coyotes, vermin, rabbits, deer, squirrels, perhaps mountain lions, and whomever I may have forgotten: I know you are all out there in the Temeculan woods. Rarely have I seen your full bodies, but daily I behold your fresh tracks sprinkling our common byways.

During my hours of daylight sauntering you are discreetly taciturn and still. Occasionally, I see one of you scurry by, sometimes I discern sounds of familiar forest-dwellers, always I sense your company.

As we uncover God only in "lurking-places" (Thoreau's insight), the same process obtains with critters of the wild, through tracks, droppings, or flitterings. And it proves enough, even holy. Moses wasn't supposed to meet God, face-to-face, lest he die. Perhaps it is best that we humans and animals espy one another obliquely as well, and that we maintain appropriate distance and decorum in our encounters.

On your behalf, my fellow beasts, I offer this fervent prayer:

> May the land stay sufficiently unspoiled and fecund to sustain you.
> May hunters die off before they take any more of you.
> May we, as human sisters and brothers, honor the rules and regulations of your territory rather than brazenly setting our own.
> Acknowledging that all wild creatures have souls, may we join one another as consorts rather than foreigners in the cosmic dance.
> May you enjoy each other's company as much as we Dorland sojourners delight in your silent, vivid traces.
> May there always be ample room in these Southern California hills to house all of you and permit occasional visits from interlopers like myself.

> Your grateful cohabitant

Ticanu Pond

No tribe of people anywhere on our continent has handled the land with greater awe and deference than the Native Americans. This entire Temecula Valley has been populated by Indians since the beginnings of Southern California civilization. The Pala, Temecula, and Pechanga tribes have roamed and settled here. Only the Pechanga Indians remain with a scattering of homes, an ancient chapel, and cemetery–a quiet reservation village sequestered in the neighboring mountains.

The hawks swoop, the wind keens, and the larks croon throughout the large grove of oak trees surrounding Ticanu Pond. Ticanu is Indian for "water of everlasting youth," but, candidly, the pond is modest, and youthful isn't exactly how one would best describe either the "fellows," "structures," or "terrain" of Dorland Mountain Arts Colony. The operative word here is "everlasting." The Ticanu setting exudes an immortal sensibility. It appears as if the oak groves and unspoiled chaparral have existed here from time immemorial.

It is reported that Ticanu is the locale of a Native American burial site. No one knows the location of the chief's grave, but it doesn't really matter. What counts is that the spirit of our native forebears be ongoingly memorialized by the way we latecomers treat this Temeculan territory.

Reverence for soil and soul is what makes Ticanu sacred. Everlasting, as they say.

Music, near and far

Why should we be in such desperate haste to succeed and in such desperate enterprises? If we do not keep pace with our companions, perhaps it is because we hear a different drummer. Let us step to the music which we hear, however measured or far away.

Thoreau

Don't come to us without bringing music.
We celebrate with drum and flute,
with wine not made from grapes,
in a place you cannot imagine.

Rumi

I am engulfed with enchanting sounds. I wander outdoors and am met by a cacophony of short, sharp chirps.

I stay inside and hear the mice at play, the rain pounding, the fire crackling, the wind howling.

I strike my singing bowl, and it emits ever-circling, sonorous waves that resonate throughout Orchard House. These bells are ancient and hand-made from the Himalayas. As I play my solitary singing bowl, I hush my mind and breathe ever so slowly and deeply.

When the sound of the bowl fades, I turn to the sounds of my own body. Sometimes the pitch of the bell resembles the primitive, universal "om" sound. Then, in prolonged fashion, I chant, "Om." The sound ricochets in my head. Extraneous noises are eliminated in the presence of "om."

I repeat this process morning, noon, and night, whenever the spirit moves me, and I remember that each day is mine to sculpt as I desire.

Sound massages and heals one.

I hum, chant, and sing simple melodies, too. Having left my conventional music-makers (guitar, tambourine, drum, and tapes) at home, I resort to the primal, human instrument: my own voice. I warm it up, air it out, then intone the round "Dona Nobis Pacem" over and over again, invoking its blessing of peace upon all life. The song comes to a natural close when we both run out of spirit. Native American wisdom rings true for me: "Song is the breath of the Spirit that consecrates the act of life." I am hallowed.

The more time I spend in the woods, the shorter my writing periods become and the longer my music-making ones, for I am possessed by Tagore's conviction: "God respects me when I work, but loves me when I sing." I am cherishing anew the sound of my own interior flute—far from any critic's pen and long after my sweet-crooning father's death. My inner instrument takes freer flight, launched from the belly, melding with the myriad voices of nature's chorus.

Music reverberates in my Dorlandian universe, "however measured or far away."

Self-massage

The woods are warming, and my early afternoon shower summons. This daily ablution unclenches the gnarled, bent parts of my body . . . and soul as well.

It was during Boy Scout summer camp in the redwoods of Northern California that I began to unfold my budding pubescence. Decades later, ensconced in the forest once again, alone this time, my flesh reawakens to touch and soaks in wanton pleasure.

Sensory exploration is like mining. The deeper one goes, wondrous crevices and caverns beyond imagining are revealed. Solitary and naked in the forest, I find myself hankering to touch objects lying around the cabin, botanical species hither and yon, and my own body, too. When no human contact, let alone embrace, is available, self-caressing blossoms. It becomes natural to fondle oneself not so much for arousal as for acknowledgment and then appreciation.

Thoreau's dictum to "explore thyself" includes bodily travels as well as spiritual excursions. An enlivening combination.

Chaparral country

A medley of shrubs
Ubiquitous, harsh thicket
Immortal garment

Far off, chaparral
Velvety-smooth curves, yielding
Up close, resistant

Stolid, evergreen oaks
Shelled nuts, decorative leaves
Hard, durable core

Ah, dwarf, scrubby oaks
Unlike fiery poppy fields
An unsung treasure

Lichen, leaping green
Lush, symbiotic algae
Beautifying rocks

Silver-plated sage
Southern Californian brush
Solemn, fragrant, wise

My manzanita
Romantic name, curvacious build
Writhes sensuously

"Wisdom . . . behold"

Love does not analyze its object.

> Journal, September 14, 1841

This curious world which we inhabit is more wonderful than it is convenient, more beautiful than it is useful—it is more to be admired and enjoyed then, than used.

> Journal, August 30, 1837

Wisdom does not inspect, but (does) behold. We must look a long time before we can see.

> Excursions, "Natural History of Massachusetts"

My rough-hewn cottage provides adequate shelter from the stormy blasts without insulating me from the sounds of the woods that seep through the semipermeable membranes, especially at nighttime. I grow sensitive to my own skin—my bark if you will—and that of the trees, plants, and animals in this natural refuge.

Today I take my afternoon walk after a sudden thunderstorm has sprayed the hills. Fresh aromas stimulate my senses—some pungent, mostly pleasant—redolent fragrances that normally go undetected back home. Thoreau warns me: "Scent is more oracular and trustworthy than eye. . . . it reveals earthiness." Life seldom seems earthier than now, after this cleansing rain.

> Southern California surliness
> Skies spitting water, dampening the soil and
>   purifying the air
> Within and without
> Preparing the wet, wild soil for exploration.

I am beholding things—gazing upon the multifarious gifts of the cosmos, scrutinizing them in minutest detail, letting them marinate in my mind's eye. Bristlingly alert, I luxuriate in these brimming sensations. My biosystem is porous to the effluence of nature.

I feel beholden, indebted to animals, shrubs, hills for the favor of their presence. They are becoming familiar to me, like family. My analytical consciousness evolves into an appreciative one.

Beholding is a mutual enterprise. The exchange goes both ways, between me and thee. An Audubon Society lady once commented to essayist E. B. White: "Mr. White, do you watch birds?" And he quickly retorted: "Yes, I do, and they watch me, too."

I behold the day with grateful pauses, having the time to relax and permitting the day to drench me with gracious surprises. My spirit is keenly attuned to the natural cycles rather than a watch or datebook.

In Thoreau's "Natural History of Massachusetts" exposition, he says that wisdom comes to us by "direct intercourse and sympathy." These words guide my journey into soul and nature: "direct," not reading about or hearing second-hand; "intercourse," literally "running between;" and "sympathy," not aloofness but affection.

"Direct intercourse and sympathy" bespeak visceral, emotional excursions rather than abstractions, and Thoreau properly chides those of us who would "explore thyself," that "no one has seen a thing who has not felt it." And I would add: "felt it physically and spiritually."

Thoreau's soul-mate, Annie Dillard, muses in a similar vein: "beauty and grace are performed in the forest whether or not we will or sense them. The least we can do is try to be there." Dillard amplifies this counsel in her trenchant volume, *Teaching the Stone to Talk,* with one of the most eloquent passages in 20th century naturalist literature:

> We are here to witness. There is nothing else to do with those mute materials we do not need. Until Larry teaches his stone to talk, until God has a change of mind, or until the pagan gods slip back to their hilltop groves, all we can do with the whole inhuman array is watch it. . . . We do not use the songbirds, for instance. We do not eat many of them; we cannot befriend them; we cannot persuade them to eat more mosquitoes or plant fewer weed seeds. We can only witness them—whoever they are. If we were not here, they would be songbirds falling in the forest. If we were not here, material events like the passage of seasons would lack even the meager meanings we are able to muster for them. The show would play to an empty house, as do all those falling stars which fall in the daytime. That is why I take walks: to keep an eye on things.

I am finally getting it through this thick skin and stubborn soul of mine that the point of life is primarily to show up, take our seats, and pay attention. The fundamental religious act is astonishment, what Rabbi Abraham Heschel called "radical amazement." If we humans "witnessed" faithfully, our ecosystem would undoubtedly flourish, and so would we.

There's a magical story about St. Francis enjoying the night air one evening in the village of Assisi. When the moon came up, it was huge and luminous and bathed the entire earth with its radiance. Noticing that no one else was outside to enjoy this miracle, Francis ran to the bell tower and began ringing the bell enthusiastically. When the people rushed from their houses in alarm and saw Francis at the top of the tower, they called out asking him to explain what was wrong. Francis replied simply, "Lift up your eyes, my friends. Lift up your eyes and look at the moon!"

So, here I am, residing in the woods, and beholding. I behold the lilies of the field. The chaparral. The vermin. The sunset. The raccoons. The wind. The stars and the moon. And the rocks—inert yet alive, too.

And the cosmos beholds me in return.

Chapter VII

Sauntering

"It is a great art to saunter"

I have met with but one or two persons in the course of my life who understood the art of Walking, that is, of taking walks—who had a genius, so to speak, for sauntering, which word is beautifully derived 'from idle people who roved about the country, in the Middle Ages, and asked charity, under pretense of going *à la Saint Terre*, to the Holy Land, till the children exclaimed, 'There goes a *Saint-Terrer*,' a Saunterer, a Holy-Lander. They who never go to the Holy Land in their walks, as they pretend, are indeed mere idlers and vagabonds; but they who do go there are saunterers in the good sense, such as I mean. Some, however, would derive the word from *sans terre*, without land or a home, which, therefore, in the good sense, will mean, having no particular home, but equally at home everywhere.

Thoreau

The saunterer is one who strolls in measured manner, with one eye on nature, the other on soul, treating the land, and all therein, as holy. The saunterer is on a sacred quest—not exercise but exploration, not recreation but *re-creation*. Sauntering is a mystical adventure. It is not the length but the depth of walk that makes it blessed.

Direction isn't paramount either, although for Thoreau the East signified the ancient treasures of European culture, whereas the West symbolized wilderness, that which remains untamed, primitive, innocent, a fairer world aching for exploration. Thoreau wrote: "Westward, I go free" and "the West of which I speak is but another name for the Wild; and what I have been preparing to say is, that in the Wildness is the preservation of the World."

Sauntering was not extraneous but indispensable to Thoreau's daily fare. He would walk in the woods up to four hours each day and he scoffed at those who considered sauntering worthless:

> If we walk in the woods for love of them half of each day, we are in danger of being regarded as a loafer; but if we spend the whole day as a speculator, shearing off those woods and making earth bald before her time, we are esteemed industrious and enterprising citizens. As if a town had no interest in its forests but to cut them down.

Nearly 150 years later the land continues to be stripped and despoiled. At our Dorland habitat, signs are posted throughout the 300 acres of natural refuge to preserve these woods for sauntering and to ward off hunters, speculators, and dirt bikers. Unfortunately, the desecrators prevail. Their trash and gun shells litter the hills.

Sauntering, along with chanting in the dark and showering in the early afternoon, has become one of my prized daily rituals at Dorland, a pleasurable way of making excursions into nature with my soul intact. As a dedicated runner for years, I intentionally have switched to walking only during my month in the woods.

I seek a clean break with the professional and physical habits of my urban existence. The shift from swift running to slow walking has proven worthwhile, but not easy. My methodical personality pressures me to move relentlessly toward a destination rather than clamber and cavort along the path as a true saunterer. Rather than pause, smell the sage, and scan the vistas, my temptation is to keep moving and gain aerobic exercise. After all, my maleness has been scripted to run my job, run my body, run my family—

run for my life.

It proves a consummate challenge for me to slow down, saunter, behold the universe outside and inside. I only now realize how driven my body and how goal-oriented my mind have been in my pre-Dorland world. Am I willing to change gears when I leave the mountains? Will I keep on sauntering or return to racing or mingle some of each?

Thoreau uses strong language in recruiting people for the great art of sauntering:

> If you are ready to leave father and mother, brother and sister, and wife and child and friends, and never see them again—if you have paid your debts, and made your will, and settled all your affairs, and are a free person, then you are ready for a walk.

To satisfy Thoreau's exhortation to "explore thyself," I had to abandon both my family and customs upon entering the hermitage of Dorland. I made a vow to pursue a different way of being self-in-the-world. But I can't measure up to Thoreau's standards. I still have some debts, and my leave-taking from loved ones is a temporary one.

There are distinctive requirements for the life of sauntering.

Although occasionally Thoreau would tolerate walking companions, he normally walked alone. He felt pestered or inconvenienced by neighbors casually asking to go on a walk with him. Sauntering is essentially a solitary endeavor. Thoreau put it bluntly: "Ask me for a certain number of dollars if you will, but do not ask me for my afternoons."

A feature of authentic sauntering is the willingness to walk in all seasons and all hours of the day or night. I qualify here, although I confess to using my flashlight at night as well as taking straightforward jaunts on well-worn paths.

Sauntering demands that we stay focused on the woods. Even

Thoreau, the ultimate saunterer, faltered at times. He admits as much:

> But it sometimes happens that I cannot easily shake off the village. The thought of some work will run in my head and I am not where my body is—I am out of my senses. In my walks I would fain return to my senses. What business have I in the woods, if I am thinking of something out of the woods?

This criterion has proven tough for me as well. My mind meanders frequently, making fleeting connections between chaparral and cottage life, forging plans, brooding over my creative output. My intention remains to divest my monkey-mind and fill my senses. When I am in the woods, I am called to *be* in the woods, not elsewhere.

Thoreau writes:

> Moreover, you must walk like a camel, which is said to be the only beast which ruminates when walking. When a traveler asked Wordsworth's servant to show him her master's study, she answered, "Here is his library, but his study is out of doors."

Quite a striking image. Ruminants are those even-toed, hooved mammals, such as sheep, giraffes, deer, and camels that chew cud repeatedly for extended periods. They are hardly the first animals to come to my mind when asked to identify with chosen beasts of the field. Yet the invitation makes sense for those who, like myself, gulp down rather than masticate experiences, hurry rather than stalk through the fields of life. Saunterers are ruminants.

One of my favorite chants while sauntering is a carefree one, a ruminator's delight. It is most appropriately chanted in blithesome fashion:

> I am moving on a journey to nowhere,
> Taking it easy, taking it slow.
> No more hurry, no more worry,
> Nothing to carry, let it all go.

Saunterers are willing to enter nature's thicket. Thoreau is direct:

> When I would recreate myself, I seek the darkest wood, the thickest and most interminable and, to the citizen, most dismal, swamp. I enter a swamp as a sacred place, a *sanctum sanctorum*. There is the strength, the marrow, of Nature.

Thoreau and I part company on this stipulation. I fear if I were to stray far from the beaten paths in the Palomar Mountains, I might get lost. I *would* get lost. Thoreau hankered for the Wild West, but, in truth, never migrated as far as the dense, impenetrable Southern California chaparral. New York, I believe, was as far westward as he ventured.

True saunterers stride in reverent, appreciative gait, treating the land, every piece of it, as hallowed, touching the earth with deft hands and with tender feet (there was nothing between Thoreau's soles and the soil except the skin of an animal). Saunterers awake, as is the Hindu custom, to caress the earth each morn, stroke it lightly, then apologize for treading upon it in the hours ahead.

The surface upon which I saunter daily is chiefly a soft compost of moistened clay sprinkled with sand and oak leaves. It is a spongy carpet which gives under my feet and springs back an amicable response. Soil and saunterer make a goodhearted, kindly pair in these woods.

It is fortifying to remember our proud lineage of saunterers and their words of wisdom as we modern women and men tread in their footsteps:

> Above all, do not lose your desire to walk: every day I walk myself into a state of well-being and walk away from every illness; I have walked myself into my best thoughts, and I know of no thought so burdensome that one cannot walk away from it.

Soren Kierkegaard, 19th century theologian

George Santayana was lecturing one morning to his philosophy class at Harvard University. After about 10 minutes, he stopped, and looking through the open windows, said to the class, "My students, it is springtime. The Earth is alive. The forsythia is in bloom and that is far, far more important than philosophy. Let us go walking."

Let children walk with Nature, let them see the beautiful blendings and communions of death and life, their joyous inseparable unity, as taught in woods and meadows, plains and mountains and streams of our blessed star, and they will learn that death is stingless indeed, and as beautiful as life... All is divine harmony.

John Muir, Scottish-born naturalist (1838-1914)

Walking is the great adventure, the first meditation, a practice of heartiness and soul; primary to humankind. Walking is the exact balance of spirit and humility. Out walking, one notices where there is food. And there are firsthand, true stories of 'Your ass is somebody else's meal'—a blunt way of saying interdependence, interconnection, ecology, on the level where it counts, also a teaching of mindfulness and preparedness.

Gary Snyder, poet

One need not travel far. To gather the benefits of wild lands, it is not necessary to bushwhack to the most remote cavern or inhospitable crag. I haven't found a correlation between spirituality and the number of miles walked.

Richard Douglas, environmental lawyer

I like to walk alone on country paths, the plants and wild grasses on both sides, putting each foot down on the earth in mindfulness, knowing that I walk on the wondrous earth. In such moments, existence is a miraculous and mysterious reality. People usually consider walking on water or in thin air a miracle. But I think the real miracle is not to walk either on water or in thin air, but to walk on earth.

Thich Nhat Hanh, Vietnamese Buddhist monk

I am a poet and a walker . . . no scientist but an explorer of the neighborhood.

Annie Dillard, writer

There are two more thoroughgoing saunterers whom I have revered: Peace Pilgrim who walked, for decades, across America as a witness for global justice and subsisted from town to town upon the support of like-minded people until her recent death; and my buddy Kent Larrabee, who spent two years sauntering across the Soviet Union on a peace mission, and, now in his seventies, returns to establish Quaker meetings in Russia as his lasting legacy for universal kinship.

Walden told of Thoreau's spiritual odyssey. This book is testament to my own soul-quest. The motifs of excursion, journey, and sauntering remain both physical and moral ones for my days ahead. When Thoreau wrote, "Be a Columbus to whole new continents and worlds within you, opening new channels, not of trade, but of thought," he was saluting the holy pilgrimage we sisters and brothers take whenever we dare to explore the unfathomable, wondrous provinces of nature and soul.

Sauntering is a great art, a way of life.

Chapter VIII

Religion

"What is religion?"

Truth is always paradoxical.

Journal, June 26, 1840

What is religion? That which is never spoken.

Journal, August 18, 1858

Our religion is where our love is.

Correspondence to Isaiah T. Williams
September 8, 1841

Being a full-fledged mystical scientist, Thoreau was continually bobbing and weaving amid the fields of paradox. Religion itself posed a persistent ambiguity for him: on the one hand, religion lies far beyond the reach of human expression; on the other, it is graphically evidenced by our deeds. In sum, religion is a blend of silence and compassion, the unsayable and the doable, mysticism and morality.

As a religious aspirant, my commitment, like Thoreau's, is to remain loyal to both poles of the paradox.

At the same time that we are earnest to explore and learn all things, we require that all things be mysterious and unexplorable, that land and sea be infinitely wild, unsurveyed and unfathomed by us because unfathomable. . . . We need to witness our own limits transgressed, and some life pasturing freely where we never wander.

Thoreau

Thoreau divulges in this passage yet another of the universe's riddles. He engages nature wholly, yet mysteries continue to abound. His grasp cannot comprehend, let alone capture, the "infinitely wild, unsurveyed and unfathomed" expanses of the cosmos.

Later in *Walden's* "Conclusion," Thoreau restates the governing principle of his cosmology. He says simply: "The universe is wider than our views of it." Note the double meaning of "views"– referring both to our sensory and philosophical perspectives.

I believe Thoreau would resonate, as I do, with D. H. Lawrence's interpretation of religion's central enigma: "Humans don't exist unless we are deeply and sensually in touch with that which can be touched but not known."

"A Transcendentalist"

The fact is I am a mystic, a transcendentalist, and a natural philosopher to boot. Now I think of it, I should have told them at once that I was a transcendentalist. That would have been the shortest way of telling them that they would not understand my explanations.

Thoreau

Thoreau was constantly at odds with the scientific establishment of his era because, in his words: " . . . they do not believe in a science which deals with the higher law." He did. As a transcendentalist, he found divine truths *within* the immanent; transcendent meanings disclosed themselves to humans inside the natural realm. He banked on intuition and believed that conscience—the inner light, the voice of God—dwelt within human beings.

Thoreau was also primarily a naturalistic mystic rather than a philosophical one; he gained entrance to the divine through sensory data rather than abstractions. As a practical transcendentalist, he alternated between ideals and facts.

Elsewhere in his journal Thoreau penned:

My desire for knowledge is intermittent; but my desire to commune with the spirit of the universe, to be intoxicated even with the fumes, call it, of that divine nectar, to bear my head through atmospheres and over heights unknown to my feet, is perennial and constant.

Clearly, Thoreau sought a wisdom higher than "knowledge"; his was a ceaseless "desire to commune with the spirit of the universe." When Emerson once bragged that most of the branches of learning were taught at Harvard, Thoreau rebutted: "Yes, indeed, all the branches and none of the roots." He spent his post-college years exploring the taproots of truth. What he didn't learn at Harvard, he surveyed in abundance at Walden Pond.

Trees

Heaven is under our feet as well as over our heads.

Thoreau

I see people as trees, walking . . .

Mark 8:24

Thoreau encourages us, like trees, to root, branch, and leaf simultaneously. This image captures the essence of his sensuous mysticism and is an apt metaphor to describe the upward and downward processes of the universe. The name "Ilan-Lael" means a tree growing, belonging to God, with its branches in the sky and its roots in the earth—spirit and matter united in form. Thoreau wrote ecstatically about these woody, majestic marvels: "The tree is as immortal as I am, and perchance will go to as high as heaven, there to tower above me still."

A tree without roots—as a people without historical continuity—topples easily. A tree is regal without being rigid. It grips hard yet is bendable to the stirrings of heavenly breeze. Our rootage as human beings must be broad and deep: broad, so we can receive nutrients from diverse sources; deep, so we sojourners can enflesh ancient symbols and stories.

Roots change, too. As the tree of our being grows taller and wider, the roots grow deeper and broader.

The trunk represents our inner identity, our core, our soul. All that happens in our lives is processed through the trunk, which links the branches above and roots below. When I examine my tree trunk, I am impelled to reflect: Where is the thickness and sturdiness in my soul?

The bark of the tree is its living, finite body. Susan Meeker-Lowry listens to the piercing lament of trees being ravaged:

> Humans, you must not falter. We trees are dying. We are not afraid of death. Death is an inevitable part of life. But we are the skin of the Earth and our children are dying, too. As we live, you live. As we die, you die.

The branches of the tree denote compassion and aspiration—reaching out to shelter and house various fellow-creatures and extending skyward in yearning and praise.

The leaves, the flowers, the fruit exemplify the seasonal shifts of our human spirit. Nature and soul both know spring, summer, fall, and winter. We blossom, we are lush, we drop leaves, we are barren.

The tree—germinal symbol and enduring presence—is our kin. Roots, trunk, bark, branches, and leaves growing up and down at once.

A wild, pertinent image comes to mind. John Muir, ardent naturalist, used to climb a tall Yosemite spruce tree during awesome thunderstorms, and would commune with the mysteries of the universe, boldly suspended, swaying vigorously back and forth between earth and heaven.

"Tonic of wildness"

We need the tonic of wildness.

Thoreau

I am an abolitionist because I am a lover of nature.

Daniel Ricketson

Thoreau heartily agreed with his friend Ricketson's position that freedom is an inherent quality of both nature and human nature. The universe in its entirety displays "the tonic of wildness." Thoreau believed only in sufficient restraints to negotiate our social contract. Anything resembling physical bondage or emotional servitude was morally offensive to him. Animals cannot be trapped and caged; neither can women and men.

As I roam the wilds of the Palomar National Forest, Thoreau reminds me to pay simultaneous homage to the unfettered, even uncivilized, territories inside our souls. He would have me cultivate, without taming, my inner beasts and unkempt terrain, as human testimony to "the tonic of wildness."

Thoreau's social activism stems from his mystical naturalism. The reason he spent a night in jail—having committed civil disobedience by refusing to pay war taxes—is philosophically interwoven with his commitment to spending 26 months' worth of nights at Walden Pond. In both cases he was obeying the call of the wild, the claims of unshackled freedom, mirrored in humans and animals alike.

Thoreau's prophetic witness was guided more by his personal leanings than the dictates of any collective, so his social deeds often baffled even close associates. As he once confided: "A brave soul will make these peaceful times dangerous, and dangerous times peaceful." Such comprised the unpredictable and often willful ethics of Henry David Thoreau.

I respectfully call the roll of those holy activists who have trod in Thoreau's footsteps, including such notables as Martin Luther King, Jr. and Dorothy Day. Like Thoreau, these individuals were equally motivated by passionate commitment to both civil protest and solitude—prophetic and contemplative demeanors, immersed in the "tonic of wildness."

Soul's geography

Waldo paid a call
The night Thoreau spent in jail
Biting wit exchanged:
"Why are you *in* there?"
cried Waldo. Henry replied:
"Why are you *out* there?

Travels far and wide
Dorland to San Diego
This tale's truth endures:
"Why are you *up* there?"
cry friends. My solo response:
"Why are you *back* there?"

Holy detachment

Do your duty without attachment to outcome.

Bhagavad Gita

A journey is a person in itself; no two are alike. And all plans, safeguards, policing, and coercion are fruitless. We find after years of struggle that we do not take a trip; a trip takes us.

John Steinbeck

"The tonic of wildness" also refers, I believe, to the art of surrendering—releasing our fist-tight control over routes and relationships. I am often bedeviled by an overweaning urge to hold sway. Dorland goads me to abandon this compulsion and to pay greater respect to the rhythms of nature beyond my dominance.

During my stay in Dorland, I am learning—sometimes with spirited struggle—to let the serendipitous enter my hours: taking a longer walk than planned, nursing the fire, drifting with a poem, playing my singing bowl on the spur of the moment, dozing off, desultory staring. Dorland summons my tight-controlling psyche to leave corners of the day and my mind wild, dangling free. As a Boy Scout I was always taught to be prepared. It is now time, in the afternoon of my life, to master the other truth of the paradox:

to be unprepared, loose, and engaged by capricious visitations. I am beginning to trust Natalie Goldberg's worldview:

> Life is not orderly. No matter how we try to make life so, right in the middle of it we die, lose a leg, fall in love, drop a jar of applesauce. In summer, we work hard to make a tidy garden, bordered by pansies with rows or clumps of columbine, petunias, bleeding hearts. Then we find ourselves longing for the forest, where everything has the appearance of disorder; yet, we feel peaceful there.

On my friend Lindy's workdesk are four printed reminders: 1) show up in your life, 2) pay attention, 3) tell the truth, and 4) let go of the outcome. The fourth is my bugaboo so I must commit to memory Thoreau's counsel: "Affect the quality of the day." He wrote "affect," not determine; influence matters somewhat without controlling them entirely. So I saunter through life, walking the high wire between being disciplined and obsessive, being a visionary and willing to relinquish my precious, hard-won visions, holding on to my loves lightly and letting go of life's outcomes.

This is no idle philosophical pastime for a card-carrying member of the so-called "sandwich generation," where, on the one hand, our children are leaving home in various states of ease or disarray and, on the other hand, our two remaining parents are sauntering, with remarkable élan, their final laps.

And I submit my soul, ever so tentatively, to the condition of holy detachment, what Thoreau called "the tonic of wildness."

Worshiping on the move

Rouse body from pew
Shout thanks unashamedly
Stroll through creation

Lift your voice in song
Hands skyward, feet gripping earth
Soaring yet grounded

Hebrews, forty years
Sojourners in wilderness
Fed on holy bread

Woods-dweller, to quest
not hunt, pluck or photograph
Wild extravagance

Untamed land within
Entangled, even barbarous
Soul's backcountry

Caught in disarray
"Solvitus ambulando"
It is solved...walking

Exploring thyself
glamorized in fantasy
Arduous journeys

"Great God Pan"

In my Pantheon, Pan still reigns in his pristine glory, with
his ruddy face, his flowing beard, and his shaggy body,
his pipe and his crook, his nymph Echo, and his chosen
daughter, Iambe; for the great God Pan is not dead, as
was rumored. Perhaps of all the Gods of New England
and of ancient Greece, I am most constant at his shrine.

Thoreau

It is no surprise that Thoreau, a full-blooded naturalist, favored the "Great God Pan." Shepherd Bliss shares mytho-poetic
reflections upon this pre-eminent pastoral deity and its special
relevance for the earthy-masculine movement today:

Pan is one of the original Wild Men—part animal, part
man, and part God. Pan is known for his erotic solitude
(some would say perversity), his distance from urban life,
and as a huntsman, dancer, leaper, and lover of the chase.
The forest and the cave were his dwellings. According to
Borgeaud, "Pan is evidently the symbolic embodiment of
the repressed. The myth seems to say: if we refuse the beast,
we shall never know how to resemble a God."

Pan, the wild, unbridled Lord of the woods, was given to
boundless mirth and swaggering sensuality. Whatever childish
joy and lustiness Thoreau displayed, he owed, in large measure,

to his acquaintanceship with Pan. Clearly Henry majored in Puritan earnestness, but on rare occasions, he exhibited his lighthearted side:

> Do they not know I can laugh? I exult in stark inanity, leering on nature and the soul. I am unworthy of the least regard, and yet I am made to rejoice. I am impure and worthless, yet the world is strewn for my delight and holidays are prepared for me, and my path is strewn with flowers. Ah, bless the Lord, O my soul! Bless him for wildness.

But Pan, a bewildering harmony of animal, human, and God, could also cast fear into the hearts of Greek travelers who, upon entering the darkest regions of the forest, experienced weird, frightful cries. Hence our word: *panic.* Nevertheless, any god worth engaging along life's path will inevitably generate a mix of delight and terror. The sportive yet grotesque Pan was no exception. Another paradox at the core of reality.

Annie Dillard adds her perspective on what she considers our god-barren, 20th-century landscape:

> God used to rage at the Israelites for frequenting sacred groves. I wish I could find one. . . . Now we are no longer primitive; now the world seems not-holy. We have drained the light from the boughs in the sacred grove and snuffed it in the high places and along the banks of the sacred streams. We as a people have moved from pantheism to pan-atheism.

Well, where does Pan fit into the religious landscape of our epoch? I offer a third theological option over against either pantheism or atheism. Instead of pantheism, a belief that equates God with everything, and atheism, a position that considers existence to be bereft of holiness, I recommend another alternative, "pan-en-theism," a viewpoint that locates the divine amid the commonplace, perceives the sacred as infusing the ordinary, and claims that the transcendent animates the immanent processes of our natural order.

I think the "transcendentalist" Thoreau would subscribe to this theological variation, although he was disinclined to label his convictions. He was loathe to quarrel with or about deity. Thoreau's only desire was to experience, not define, God. Nonetheless, the following anecdote told of Henry as a young child, augurs early *pan-en-theistic* inclinations:

> When his mother found him still awake in bed she asked, "Why, Henry dear, why don't you go to sleep?" "Mother," said he, "I have been looking through the stars to see if I couldn't see God behind them."

The rest of his life Thoreau searched for and found the divine "through the stars," embedded, as it were, in the flow of the natural domain.

Pan-en-theism holds that the Creator is discernible in but not exhausted by the plants, animals, humans of creation. It makes room for the mystery of soul, the unfathomableness of nature, the wholly "otherness" of God.

I remember leading a children's worship service years back. Kindergarten through sixth-grade children were gathered in a beautiful chapel setting. We were conversing about God, a most ticklish theological term for adults, let alone kids.

One of the older children, a bright sixth grader, rose to her feet and with immense self-assurance, if not cockiness, uttered: "I think that God is a *force!*" She spoke with such imperiousness that discussion promptly ceased. The little ones in the room gazed up at the sixth grader in glowing adoration, as if to concede that God's nature was definitively revealed. Only adults and God itself could be larger, in their eyes, than this budding teenager.

Then one of our irrepressible five-year-olds broke the silence and boldly blurted out, "Hey, I saw a *forest* once!"

Then with an immense smile on my face, and even greater one in my heart, I reached out to recognize both the gifts of the big child and the little one and all sizes in between gathered in our Chapel. And these words tumbled forth from my belly: "Yes, children, God is a force who can be found in the forest and oh, so many other neat and wild places as well."

Socrates' prayer in Plato's *Phaedrus*, one of the simplest, most expressive prayers in all of literature, captures the enduring religious drive to commune with nature and explore one's soul in the company of Pan:

> Beloved Pan, and all ye other gods who haunt this place, give me beauty in the inward soul; and may the outward and inward be as one.

Three cheers and a whole host of hallelujahs to the Great God Pan, Thoreau's divine friend, an enduring Force in the Forest.

"Let God alone"

Let God alone if need be. Methinks, if I loved him more, I should keep him—I should keep myself rather—at a more respectful distance. It is not when I am going to meet God, but when I am just turning away and leaving God alone, that I discover that God is. I say, God. I am not sure that that is the name.

Thoreau

God does not speak prose, but communicates with us by hints, omens, inferences, and dark resemblances in objects around us.

Ralph Waldo Emerson

These are provocative passages for Western ideologists who thrive on harnessing God for our own ends. All machinations to the contrary, God remains a slippery, evasive reality. In fact, God is the word we humans use, but that isn't necessarily God's name at all.

Animals need space to roam wild. Humans need to remain unfettered on the pathway toward enlightenment. God is no different. God covets private space. Like running water, God hankers to flow free and natural. C.S. Lewis wrote: "You can't tame God, who's wild, you know."

D.H. Lawrence confessed in a similar vein:

> This is what I believe:
> That my soul is a dark forest,
> That my known self will never be
> more than a clearing in the forest,
> That gods, strange gods, come
> forth from the forest
> into the clearing of my known self,
> and then go back,
> That I must have the courage to
> let them come and go.

But we covetous, grasping humans won't let God come and go. We vainly try to domesticate the Eternal. We attempt to manipulate the Unknowable with sanctimonious, self-serving prayers. We shrink the Creator to bumper stickers and lampshade slogans. We harm other humans and wreak havoc with earth all under the guise of "serving" our puny, parochial deities.

Thoreau urges us to calm down, back off, maintain a "more respectful distance" from the Source of all existence. If we would truly honor the Great Spirit, if we would enter the Great Silence with praise and thanksgiving, then let us allow God to be God, to be alone.

With a playful yet cutting touch, Thoreau recommends that if humans are really desperate for fellowship, we should spend our time befriending the devil: "God is alone—but the devil, he is far from being alone; he sees a great deal of company; he is legion."

Paradox activates the religious pilgrim once more. When we don't pressure, even pursue, God, when we let God alone . . . the divine presence is likely to pay an unexpected visit. Is it any surprise that alone, we may meet the Alone? Or, when on the trail, engrossed in reflection or observation, we may run into Pan? Ironically, one so intimate with Yahweh as Moses "went up on Mt. Sinai, waited still in a cleft of the rock and saw the back parts of God." (Exodus 33:22-23) Backparts or frontparts, God will meet us in God's own time and fashion.

This is why Thoreau writes in his Journal:

> My profession is to be always on the alert to find God in nature, to know his lurking-places, to attend all the oratorios, the operas, in nature.

The divine presence skulks, stays hidden, lurks in the furtive recesses of soul and nature. As explorers of the Creation we are summoned to saunter about fully awake and to stalk the Holy in enchanted haunts.

Chapter IX

Peace

Today is a very good day to die.
Every living thing is in harmony with me.
Every voice sings a chorus within me.
All beauty has come to rest in my eyes.
All bad thoughts have departed from me.
Today is a very good day to die.
My land is peaceful around me.
My fields have been turned for the last time.
My house is filled with laughter.
My children have come home.
Yes, today is a very good day to die.

                                    Nancy Woods

Pleasure and peace

I hear a good many pretend that they are going to die; or that they have died for aught I know. Nonsense! I defy them to do it. They haven't got life enough in them. . . . Only a half a dozen or so have died since the world began.

Thoreau

After staying out on a December morn counting tree rings in the sleet, Thoreau caught the cold that eventuated in his death. He met his demise doing what he loved most in the woods so dear to him.

We often remark, "What a wonderful day it is to be alive!" Whenever we awake in the morning, fully present, with few regrets, enmeshed in the nobler activities of the soul, we could equally exclaim, "What a wonderful day on which to die!"

Sam Staples, once Thoreau's jailer, came to visit Henry near his death and told Emerson afterwards: "Never spent an hour with more satisfaction; never saw someone dying with so much pleasure and peace."

Henry David Thoreau died as he lived.

"I never knew we quarreled"

When Aunt Louisa, staunch Calvinist to the bitter end, asked her nephew if he had made peace with God, Thoreau replied that he was unaware that they had ever quarreled. Neither an ardent nor conventional religionist, Henry David Thoreau lived a brief but fulfilled existence (44 years), truthful to his convictions, in harmony with "the higher laws" as he perceived them, and in genial kinship with the Great God Pan.

He never boasted of his relationship with any God. He didn't banter or debate about deity. He was shy even discussing the subject. Thoreau was solely devoted to experiencing God first-hand in the depths of psyche and plenitude of creation.

Bronson Alcott noted:

> I always think of Thoreau when I look at a sunset. . . . He said to me in his last illness, "I shall leave the world without regret." That was the saying either of a grand egotist or of a deeply religious soul.

I prefer the latter designation—"a deeply religious soul." Thoreau didn't seem at grave odds with his limited yet special chamber in the cosmos. He found little cause to quarrel with God.

Hence he left "the world without regret," offering his final goodbyes and surrendering contentedly to the endless sleep.

"One world at a time!"

His friend and fellow abolitionist Parker Pillsbury called upon Thoreau wanting to talk about the afterlife, a topic of substantial interest to Pillsbury, especially being a former minister. Hoping to coax out some clearer vision of the world to come, Pillsbury pressed: "You seem so near the brink of the dark river, that I almost wonder how the opposite shore may appear to you, Henry."

The wily Thoreau quipped, "One world at a time! One world at a time!"

Thoreau gave his fullest self to the present moment, this natural world, the only one he knew, the home he cared about—"the real, solid, sincere" terrain of corporeal existence. He left matters concerning the next realm totally up to the Creator.

In eulogizing his dead friend, Emerson turned away from Thoreau's fresh grave, muttering, "He had a beautiful soul, he had a beautiful soul!"

Louisa May Alcott confirmed the mission of Thoreau's life in her fitting farewell:

> It seemed as if Nature wore her most benignant aspect to welcome her dutiful and loving son to his long sleep in her arms. As we entered the church yard birds were singing, early violets blooming in the grass and the pines singing their softest lullaby, and there between his father and his brother we left him, feeling that though his life seemed too

short, it would blossom and bear fruit for us long after he was gone, and that perhaps we should know a closer relationship now than even while he lived.

Soul *and* nature. Soul *in* nature.

Epilogue

I left the woods for as good a reason as I went there. Perhaps it seemed to me that I had several more lives to live, and could not spare any more time for that one...

Thoreau

Later in his Journal, Thoreau confided that he didn't know precisely why he left Walden Pond when he did:

I have often wished myself back. . . . Perhaps if I lived there much longer, I might live there forever.

In any case, he departed after two years, two months, and two days, and although he returned home to Concord, his Walden experiment was unalterably recorded in his memory—moreover, in his ensuing behavior. The woods stayed in Thoreau's soul.

The remainder of his life he honored the same compelling fusion of mystical bent and outdoorsmanship. He never fully acclimated to society; he was incurably a child of nature. He continued to write in the mornings and to take lengthy walks in the afternoon. He left evenings vacant for reading and conversation.

My re-entry varies from Thoreau's. I return to a family, professional life, and a multitude of social obligations and moral quandaries. But my soul has thickened, and my bond with nature strengthened. I will be sauntering more now, whether at work or in the woods, at home or play.

> I learned this, at least, by my experiment; that if one advances confidently in the direction of one's dreams, and endeavors to live the life one has imagined, one will meet with a success unexpected in common hours. One will put some things behind, will pass an invisible boundary; new, universal, and more liberal laws will begin to establish themselves around and within oneself; or the old laws will be expanded, and interpreted in one's favor in a more liberal sense and one will live with the license of a higher order of beings.
>
> Thoreau

I would be as brazen as Thoreau and claim some already-derived success from my rudimentary excursions into nature and soul. My vision will never revert to its original size. "New, universal, and more liberal laws" are taking root. "My experiment" has been of immeasurable worth, and I have barely begun to unravel its benefits.

I live with "the license of a higher order of beings." I like "beings" in the plural here, because I am definitely not alone upon my return. I left the woods residing in the spiritual company of Thoreau and others, including animals and plants newly befriended. This entire lot travel back home with me.

I quickly and quietly vacated the Mountain Arts Colony with

a bevy of fresh acquaintances, mainly of the nonhuman variety. I had cautiously entered what Wendell Berry calls "the peace of wild things." I grew a closer friendship with my solitariness, quiet and calm, engulfed in the sensitive warm-cold, light-dark rhythms of winter in the Southern California wilds.

I introduced myself to the muse, venturing into the Eastern genre of poetry known as Haiku, an imaginative mode of giving voice to my inner and outer discoveries.

I read *myself* far more regularly than *others*, although I cannot match Thoreau's exceptional early stretch at Walden: "I did not read books the first Summer; I hoed beans."

I spent abundant meditative time, greeting both angels and demons on a more intimate basis, assisted by my talking stick and singing bowl. These spiritual practices will weave their way into my tomorrows.

Chanting carried me to places essentially foreign yet remarkably serene. I centered upon three basic plainsongs.

1) "Earth, wind, water and fire . . . return, return, return, return" is an earth-centered, pagan chant which tethered me tightly with nature, even as I vocalized quietly inside Orchard House.

2) Then there was Harry Belafonte's calypso piece: "I come from the mountain, living in the mountain, go back to the mountain, turn the world around." As I inserted various locations for "mountain" like ocean, valley, city, church, family, whatever, I was struck by the song's clarion call for us to return to our origins and embody *there* the soul-work initiated away from home. In so doing, our multiple, intersecting worlds might be transformed.

3) One final chant—"Listen, listen, listen to my heart's song; listen, listen, listen to my heart's song; I will never for-

sake you, I will never forget you; I will never forsake you, I will never forget you"—has been familiar to me for years.

Its meanings reverberate in my soul. Even when I am long gone and far way from Dorland I will neither forsake its learnings nor forget its legacy. I will remember Ticanu Pond eternally. Such is my heart's song, my life promise.

Thoreau wrote at the conclusion of his Walden excursion:

If you have built castles in the air, your work need not be lost; that is where they should be. Now put the foundations under them.

There is no guru or deity around, Thoreau or Pan included, who will enforce faithfulness to my pledge. It's up to me to build the proper foundations under my Dorlandian "castles," to keep its flame burning in my soul.

As I mentioned in the introduction, Thoreau and I have not been alone in our pilgrimages. An exemplary host of companions have also experienced the cycles of entrance into the woods and return to the community.

Gautama, when he was twenty-nine years old, withdrew into the forest, seeking enlightenment, and when he found it, returned among the people and shared his wisdom. To put his life in perspective, Buddha withdrew for six years; he returned for 45 years.

Jesus, when he was 30 years old, at the start of his ministry, retreated into the desert, then reentered society to preach his good news, for three full years, up until his death.

During his ministry Jesus sought the solace of companionship in hours of spiritual stress. So he took a few of his closest friends with him whenever he went away for days of quiet recuperation. "Come ye apart and rest awhile," he said. Yet Jesus was usually alone, secluded from even his closest comrades. His life ended with a lonely vigil in a garden followed by the cross. There was something starkly solitary about Jesus. As the spiritual goes, "Jesus walked this lonesome valley, he had to walk it by himself." So do we.

The four Hindu growth stages for the spiritual pilgrim are student, householder, and forest-dweller, followed occasionally by the state of *sannyasin,* described by the Bhagavad Gita as "one who neither hates nor loves anything." The sannyasin appears utterly free, likened by the Hindus to a wild goose or swan, comfortable, at peace, everywhere.

I can't, nor would I wish to, claim the state of sannyasin. I am too young and far too short of wisdom or serenity. Yet my transition from the forest back to the marketplace is not unlike that of myriad pilgrims before me. I return to my metropolitan home as gracefully and gratefully as possible, heeding all the while the admonition of Sister Maria Jose Hobday:

> And my mother would tell me: "Take this beauty into your heart; learn it. Some day you will be far from here, and you will only be able to see this with the eyes of your heart. Then it will be important for you to have the beauty inside you. Memorize the land."

I would memorize the land of Ticanu Pond and preserve it for my interior visits. I am mindful of Thoreau's example: "I keep a mountain anchored off eastward a little way, which I ascend in my dreams both awake and asleep. . . . I keep this mountain to ride instead of a horse."

I believe in keeping imaginary mountains operative in my daily dreaming and in holding Dorland's real forest indelibly printed in my spirit's vision. I will need all the mountains and woods at my disposal for life's homestretch.

But, I'm afraid, there is other advice I cannot in good conscience follow. It is John Muir's: "To get these glorious works of God into yourself–that's the thing; not to write about them!" I reply to this eminent naturalist: "It's not an either-or proposition, my colleague, but a both-and. I will ingest the 'works of God' *and* write about them. I must relate the story of my simple journeys into nature and soul."

Thoreau couldn't restrain his pen either:

Is not the poet to write his own biography? Is there any other work for him but a good journal?

Good writing and noble living are inextricably intertwined. Writing never does full justice to the original events, but it does preserve the memory and pass on the torch. John Muir knew that as well; that's why he couldn't follow his own advice. He turned out to be a splendid, prolific writer.

So, here's my journal, replete with holes and smudges, revised over a five-year period, a "simple and sincere account" of my sauntering in the woods with Thoreau.